HEROES OF POPULAR CULTURE

HEROES OF POPULAR CULTURE

EDITED BY

Ray B. Browne
Marshall Fishwick
Michael T. Marsden

Bowling Green University Popular Press
Bowling Green, Ohio 43403

ART CREDITS:

Cover design by Caroline Baker and Richard Charnigo.

Art work by Richard Charnigo.

Contents

R. Charango

By MARSHALL FISHWICK
Prologue

In the days of Eisenhower the Conqueror, the valley stood so fat with corn that they laughed and sang. Content in one of those havens—the Valley of Virginia—I wrote of American heroes. Ah yes, I remember it well.

And if I forget, I can re-read *American Heroes, Myth and Reality* (1953), written in a room overlooking the chapel where my favorite hero, Robert E. Lee, was buried. Lee, the noble knight, above reproach; looking back to Washington's Crusade to free the colonies, looking forward to Eisenhower's Crusade to free Europe. A few blocks away another noble knight, "Stonewall" Jackson (the Patton of the Civil War) lay buried. Everything fit, every hero was linked in the Great Chain of Being—back in 1953 A.D.

This book attempts to find out what has happened to the American hero—and thus to America—since then.

Exit Eisenhower, enter Kennedy. Suddenly everything was popping: empires, ideologies, arts, ghettoes, population, platitudes. Cold wars got hot, kids became cool, and God was said to be dead. Suddenly, a counterculture, shouting its barbaric yawp from the roof-tops of Academia, was turning every period into a question mark.

1

So of course the heroic style—masquerading often as anti-heroic—changed too. Ugly became beautiful, odd became even. The key word was neither realistic nor romantic but psychedelic; not oral or verbal but multi-sensory; not improvised or planned but electronic. Pop went the hero.

Suddenly my old crop—not only the 18th century swashbucklers, squires, and cavaliers, but also the 19th century frontiersmen, self-made men, and industrial tycoons—looked archaic. (The "in" word was irrelevant.) Even the presidency looked different when Kennedy occupied it: first born in the 20th century, first to emerge from the political vortex of megalopolis, first Roman Catholic. Moreover, he refused to be "official" and "corny." Like a good jazz musician, he knew the power of flatting and deflating. When asked how he became a hero when the Japanese attacked in World War II, he answered: "They sank my boat."

He abhorred sentiment, purple prose, and platitudes. His careful exploitation of mass media was a hallmark; his press conferences were masterpieces of relaxed, confident exposition. Here was the old F.D.R. "Fireside Chat" adapted for TV by Prince Charming.

That is why Kennedy's assassination, in 1963, is the most crucial event in the heroic history of our generation. Because of the times and technology, Kennedy had a global popularity unlike that of any other president, or of any man then alive. That he should be killed senselessly by an ex-Marine, who was in turn killed on television before millions of viewers, still forms an unbelievable historic episode—a happening.

This sense of the unexpected, the unbelievable, was flavored with a tang of the grotesque. As in a mixed-up movie, in which the film ran backwards, we found ourselves in 1964 watching Barry Goldwater campaigning for the presidency on horseback. Old timers who remembered Buffalo Bill were filled with nostalgia. Not so for most Americans. Even a Texas Ranger seemed better than this. Lyndon B. Johnson, the last of the 19th century presidents, took office.

The Johnson Years, like all others, mirror the knotty and perennial American paradoxes: Virgin Land *vs.* Raped Landscape; Arcadia *vs.* Grub City; consensus *vs.* anarchy; citadel *vs.* caravan. Some sat in while others sold out. A single catalytic agent, Viet Nam, changed oldstyle American military heroes into newstyle villains. Caught between the corncob and the computer, Middle America didn't know whether to go back to the farm or forward to the moon.

There was no national mourning when a contemporary of John F. Kennedy—Woody Guthrie—died in 1967. Yet Guthrie was a proto-popular hero who would be reincarnated in a talented imitator, Bob Dylan, and Woody's less talented son, Arlo. The ghost of Guthrie, as much as that of Kennedy, haunts the pages of this anthology.

Left alone with his young brother in an Oklahoma shanty, Woody was an orphan of living parents. Most of his life was spent in compulsive, aimless rambling. Yet he left a body of work—over a thousand songs—which document his whole period. "Some of them are purty dern left-handed," Guthrie admitted. "They are so left wing, I had to write 'em with my left hand and sing 'em with my left tonsil." Along with more learned contemporaries whom he never read or quoted—the Existentialists—Guthrie helped to put anti-hero on the center of the stage. So did Norman Mailer, who gradually emerged as the prototype author of his generation. Going through many changes after writing his best-selling novel about World War II (*The Naked and the Dead*) Mailer mirrored the cataclysmic changes that followed. His *credo* was clearly stated in *Advertisements for Myself:*

> The decision is to encourage the psychopath in one-self; to explore that domain of experience where security is boredom and therefore sickness; to exist in that enor-mous present which is without past or future, memory or planned intention.

The heroic hobo was popular again. The word, thought to be derived from "Ho, boy," had been used for a century to describe homeless and penniless vagrants who first travelled the rails, then the roads. Strong backers of the Populist Revolt in the 1890's (did we re-stage the election of 1896 in 1972?) then of the Wobblies labor movement, the hoboes have long sung their heady, irresponsible songs:

> Hallelujah, I'm a bum!
> Hallelujah, bum again,
> Hellelujah! Bum a handout,
> Revive me again. [1]

The new King of the Road was Jack Kerouac, whose best-seller was called, appropriately, *On the Road.* This errant prodigal son from the Roman Catholic Church went on to write *Dharma Bums, Visions of Gerard,* and *The Subterraneans.*   In his wake came the Hippies, city and politics-oriented, more anxious to do than to write. For them liberty, equality, and fraternity became turn on, tune in, and drop out. For thousands of Americans "finding myself" meant "freaking out." A whole new vocabulary of drug addiction cropped up. Often their protest was scattered and controllable: but not at the 1968 Chicago Democratic Convention, or on the campus of Kent State in Ohio.

Historians stress that unheroic or anti-heroic characters are deeply rooted in the past—fool, clown, scapegoat, freak, rebel without a cause, angry young man. But never before have they been full-blown authentic popular American heroes, pushing the oldstyle knights, generals, and moneymakers off the stage. At least so it seemed, on the surface; but were the old heroes destroyed or transformed? Were we not still entranced by what James Joyce calls in *Finnegan's Wake* a monomyth? Are our new popular heroes—sometimes, like Nanki-Poo in *The Mikado,* disguised as second trombones —brand new or retreads? Do they not re-enact the old rites of passage: separation, initiation, return? Do they not venture forth still from the world of common dullness to the region of fleeting wonder?[2]

The heroic scene is changing too rapidly, and we are too close to it, to give final answers to long-range questions. We *can* say that changes in media, lifestyle, priorities, ideologies will be reflected in our heroes. Motion pictures and television confer celebrity, for example—not just on people, but on art objects, places, ways of life. Everything is visible with the Big Eye; ethnic groups which were once under-viewed are now seen and discussed far out of proportion to their numerical strength in the total culture. Indians and Blacks wage large-scale campaigns against traditional American heroes. Writing of "The White Race and Its Heroes" in *Soul on Ice,* Eldridge Cleaver sees more need for shame than pride in our heroic past:

> That such venerated figures as George Washington and
> Thomas Jefferson owned hundreds of black slaves . . . and
> that every president since Lincoln connived politically and
> cynically with the issues affecting the human rights of most
> American people—these facts weigh heavily upon the hearts
> of the white youth.

His sneers at "Mr. & Mrs. Yesterday" have been repeated and

echoed for a decade. Not only flesh-and-blood writers, but printer's-ink comic characters, have altered. Consider Superman. Created in the Depression as an icon, restlessly eager to embrace violent solutions, he has become alienated and disillusioned. Standing on top of a skyscraper, looking at ant-like humans below, he muses: "For the first time in many years I feel that I'm alone . . ."

Even Superman isn't as alienated as a 1969 group chronicled in *Esquire*. Called the Chickenshits, they wore yellow armbands, carried a yellow flag, and played kazoos. When confronted by opposition, they dropped to the floor and crawled out mumbling, "Grovel, grovel, grovel, who are we to ask for power? "[3]

"Ask for it—who wants it?" Joyce Maynard queried three years later in a widely-quoted *New York Times* article called, "An 18-Year Old Looks Back on Life" (April 23, 1972). "Everyone is raised on nursery rhymes and nonsense stories," she concluded. "But it used to be that when you grew up, the nonsense disappeared. Not for us." Will her popular heroes believe this too?

One notes that the anti-heroes or reluctant heroes remain strong in the 1970's. Their admirers and chroniclers are proud to repeat what Craig McGregor, a devoted Dylanologist, says about Bob Dylan: "He is both anti-political and anti-intellectual. He is a Three-Minute-Twelve track-Super-acrylic-Longplay-Hero with an automatic cutoff at the song's end."[4] Is that any way to run Olympus?

Why scrutinize and lionize the anti-hero? Because, the argument generally runs, he enacts the dilemmas and crises of the generation he represents. Thus, Dylan has taken us through politics, drugs, transcendentalism, communes, love . . . "What the hell else have we a right to ask of him?"

Or to ask of Janis Joplin (1943-1970), our Right-Here-and-Now Do-It-Baby who tried everything—including suicide? Fashionably famous for her work with a San Francisco group called Big Brother and the Holding Company, she was quoted as saying: "I don't know what happened. I just exploded."[5] Don Heckman called her a study in tension—beads, fringe, and hair streaming in every direction, her hands constantly moving, like curiously delicate butterflies; drinking, cursing, crying, sometimes all at the same time. She was under thirty when she joined Jean Harlow, James Dean, Jackson Jimi Hendrix, and Marilyn Monroe in the Cult of the Early Dead. "Janis designed her own package," her Mother concluded, "and the package became the person."

Yet neither Marilyn Monroe nor Janis Joplin is heroine of one of the major movements of our time—Women's Liberation. How can there be a book of heroes without heroines? Where in this vast subject do we accommodate such historic heroic figures as Sarah Moore Grimke, Lucretia Mott, Elizabeth Cady Stanton, Susan B. Anthony, Carrie Catt, and Eleanor Roosevelt? "I ask no favors for my sex," Sarah Grimke wrote in 1838. "All I ask of our brethren is that they take their feet from off our necks."

That the new woman may reenact old patterns is suggested in Jerome Rodnitzky's "A Pacifist St. Joan: The Odyssey of Joan Baez." In the final essay of his new collection called *Representative Men· Cult Heroes of Our Time* (Collier-Macmillan, 1970), Theodore L. Gross includes a piece on Jacqueline Onassis, whom he labels "The Existential Heroine," a queen deprived of court and clout. Nothing here to delight or inspire Gloria Steinem; but then, Mr. Gross does dedicate the book to his Mother.

As with so many contemporary areas, the relationship between hero and heroine is not clearly defined or understood. Some would chalk up to male chauvinism Paul O'Neil's concluding that "Jackie was going to have her cake and eat it, too, and all without being beholden."[6] Therefore we must plan (under feminine editorship) a book on HEROINES OF POPULAR CULTURE before expecting the sexless anthology.

Such a book would acknowledge that some of the most admired females of our time have paid little attention to Women's Lib. As Jerome Rodnitzky points out, Joan Baez has little sympathy with either female or black liberation movements, which divide rather than join people. To her the only relevant question is: "How do we stop men from murdering each other?"

What emerges time after time, from these essays and other studies of the hero, is that the field has become fluid instead of static; dominated by images rather than words. Since we have instant information, we expect instant action. Faced with instant problems, we look for leaders with instant solutions. In this sense, the hero of the 1970's (whatever his field) must be a performer. A host of crucial questions follow. Why do we both demand and destroy "stars"? How do great performers turn routine appearances into "unique acts"? Is performance always a means, or can it also be an end?

It may well be that a generation which is better educated, more sophisticated, more travelled and media-exposed than any in history will demand and expect more from heroes. Because no highly pub-licized figure can any longer hide his contradictions, shortcomings, and recorded blunders, the old one-dimensional hero or paragon is finished. We have to accept the new crop warts and all, or not at all. Might this be one cause of the anti-hero trend?

Thus, one has to accept the contradictions inherent in a figure like Cassius Clay (alias: "The Lip" and "Gasseous Cassius") who changed his name to Mohammed Ali. Not only does he combine very different physical and spiritual attributes; he also moves beyond the role of boxer, to become a poet, philosopher, critic. We see his dis-parities in life; for Marilyn Monroe, they emerged only in death. The stereotyped "dumb blonde" was actually a tragic figure; she knew and she cared very much. And what do you make of the multiple roles of a Bill Cosby, Jane Fonda, Joe Namath, Dick Gregory, or Richard Nixon?

We know far too little about the juxtaposition of public images and the impact of constant media-exposure on those who fascinate and inspire us. Only by responding to the public's insatiable passion for poetic stimulation can the hero remain "on top." No wonder frauds and deceptions are practiced and condoned. The crime, Sid Robinovitch has suggested in his study of symbols and celebrities, is not against people but against language.

We hope we have sinned against neither people nor language in assembling these essays on popular heroes. We have chosen only a few from multitudes, and without any logical or philosophical for-mat. Nor are we prepared to defend to the death the figures we have chosen. By the time these words are in print, some new heroes will have arrived, and some that seem bright today will have faded. That is the limitation, strength, and fascination of our subject.

As Norman Mailer—writer, stud, film-maker, popular hero—points out, "America is a country which has grown by the leap of one hero past another." That process can be confusing and deceptive. Fact can blend with fancy, truth with fiction. That too is part of the territory. "Who cares what the fact was," asked Ralph Waldo Emerson, "when we have made a constellation of it to hang in heaven, an immortal sign?"

NOTES

[1]From *The Hobo's Hornbook: A Repertory for a Gutter Jongleur*, George Milburn, editor (New York, Washburn, 1930). See also Kenneth Allsop, *Hard Travellin': The Hobo and His History* (New York, New American Library, 1968).

[2]This, at least, is the chief argument of Joseph Campbell in *The Hero With a Thousand Faces* (New York, Meridian, 1956).

[3]Gary Willis, "The Making of Yippie Culture, *Esquire*, Nov., 1969, pp. 135 f.

[4]Craig McGregor, "Dylan: Reluctant Hero of the Pop Generation," New York *Times*, May 7, 1972. Adapted from a forthcoming critical anthology entitled *Bob Dylan: A Retrospective*.

[5]Don Heckman, "Janis Joplin," New York *Times*, October 11, 1972.

[6]Paul O'Neil, "For the Beautiful Queen Jacqueline, Goodby Camelot, Hello Skorpios," reprinted by Theodore Gross, *op. cit.*, pp. 526 f.

By MARSHALL FISHWICK
Heroic Style in America

America's heroic style evades chronology, but not contour. We assign the swashbuckler to the seventeenth century only to have Doug Fairbanks leap onto the twentieth-century scene, sword in hand. We think we've seen the last of the cavaliers who sat proudly on their horses and dashed toward Gettysburg—only to find General Patton atop his tank turret, dashing toward Germany. Fairbanks and Patton inherited their style from earlier epochs of swashbucklers and cavaliers. They reflect contours of an earlier time, as the rear-view mirror reflects the landscape behind.

Other heroes anticipate epochs yet to come. Cool ones dominate the twentieth century; but there was also something wonderfully cool about sixteenth-century Sir Francis Drake, "singeing the beard of the Spanish king" by sailing right into the harbor at Cadiz, or laconic, eccentric, professor-turned-Civil-War-soldier "Stonewall" Jackson, saying quietly to his aides, "If the enemy is still standing at sunset, press them with the bayonet." The history of heroes echoes and re-echoes statements and styles down the corridors of time.

In that history, repetition and revolution exist side by side. The red badge of courage for today's youth is long hair; nothing signals popstyle more decisively. Old boys moan the new barbarism and shagginess in the same terms as did Thomas Hall in 1654:

9

> Go, Gallants, to the Barbers go
> Bid them your hairy Bushes mow.
> God in a Bush did once appear
> But there is nothing of Him here.[1]

What the newly emerging bushy-headed hero stands for, no one can yet say. He is not, Ihab Hassan notes, exactly the liberal's idea of the victim, nor the conservative's idea of the outcast, nor the radical's idea of the rebel. He finally appears as an expression of man's quenchless desire to affirm, despite the pressures of our age, the human sense of life.[2]

Some of America's most colorful paragons were heroes in homespun—products of a genuine, orally transmitted folklore that did not scorn the grass-roots idiom:

> Beefsteak when I'm hungry,
> Corn likker when I'm dry,
> Pretty little gal when I'm lonesome,
> Sweet heaven when I die.

Diligent collectors have found examples of ballads, dance and game lyrics, blues, spirituals, work songs, hymns and white spirituals, Indian chants and prayers, trickster tales, local legends, tall tales, adapted European stories. There is no shortage in America of superstitions, sayings, proverbs, occupational jokes, and an infinite variety of games, dances, riddles, and rhymes. The distilled experience of generations of birth, life, and death are universal themes with local habitations and names.

What changes is locale, personnel, circumstances. In America the hero moved steadily westward, until he reached Hollywood. Later, he went into orbit. Popular favorites advanced from the open forest to the big tent to the nightclub to the discotheque. European oldstyle was left behind as American folkstyle took root in the rich virgin land. Farmer-planters like Thomas Jefferson, George Washington, and William Penn set our pattern in politics. The myth of the garden, summarized at the end of the nineteenth century by Frederick Jackson Turner, coupled with the Jeffersonian ideal of the family farm to provide the chief theme of American history. Karl Marx also used the struggle between country and city as a major theme in *Das Kapital.* Simultaneously, American ballad-makers complained:

> The farmer is the man
> Lives on credit till the fall;

Then they take him by the hand
And they lead him from the land
And the city man's the man who gets it all.

What happened to the country man in a rapidly changing economy is paralleled by the history of one of his best-loved songs, "Home on the Range." Written by Brewster Highley in 1873, it was picked up as a folksong by John A. Lomax in 1908. In the 1930's city people made it into a popular "hit." The politicians turned Brewster Highley's log cabin, where he allegedly wrote the song, into a shrine. By then, rural sociologists acknowledged that their field had virtually ceased to exist.[3]

So had the traditional ballads, full of oldstyle and folkstyle heroes. In earlier form they had been handed down from the past without known individual authorship; showed evidence of variation in content; had a compact and concise narrative; made much of repetition and refrain.[4] Instead of going to such native folk material, early American writers preferred to return to European precedents. Washington Irving, the first widely accepted professional American writer, made a fairyland of the Hudson Valley by importing tales from the Rhine, changing distant Otmar into nearby Rip Van Winkle.[5] In so doing he became a founding father of American fakestyle, which eventually over-shadowed both oldstyle and folkstyle.

Fakestyle impetus also came directly from Europe, where the "artsy-craftsy" ideas of Neo-Medievalists like John Ruskin and William Morris enjoyed a wide vogue. Hatred of early machine civilization, best exemplified in their native England, caused them to retreat to mythical Camelot—a kingdom John F. Kennedy would covet in the twentieth century. While the English were condemning machines, Americans were using theirs to produce dime novels and give fakestyle an enormous boost. The key date here is June 1860, when the first example of this new vulgarism, a uniquely American form of popular literature, was published. This sensational "yellowback," written by Ann S. Stephens, was entitled *Malaeska: The Indian Wife of the White Hunter.* Soon Beadle's New Dime Novels, Frank Starr's American Novels, and the Beadle-Adams combination changed the nation's reading habits. Folkstyle is built on facts and real events, fakestyle on images and pseudo-events. We have seen how fakestyle changed America's heroes.

The 1876 Philadelphia World's Fair gave fakestyle another

boost. Exhibits stressed the production of bijouterie—"artistic" bronzes, luxurious furniture, and artificial flowers that had (to quote the French critic Simonin) "the veritable stamp of solidity and good taste." A key statistic involves the sale of jigsaw blades in America, chief source of bric-a-brac and fretwork. About 3,000 a year were sold in 1875—over 500,000 a month in 1878.[6]

"Americans," William Dean Howells complained, "have cast about for the instruction of someone who professed to know better, and who browbeat wholesome commonsense into the self-distrust that ends in sophistication." As if to illustrate his claim, the lead article in *Harper's Bazaar* for July 1, 1876, urged readers to clip items out of periodicals, then paste them "in a pretty scrap album for the library table. Stick on all sorts of little ornaments: monograms, little gilt devices cut from envelope bands, false flowers— anything at all that is pretty."[7]

While ladies were clipping for scrapbooks and Robber Barons were bringing home European art objects by the barrel-load, the era's greatest American writer was still drawing from folk material. Born in a sordid frontier town, schooled in mining camps and riverboat pilothouses, Mark Twain created the last genuinely American folk hero, *Huckleberry Finn*. In presenting Huck, he also showed that a novel could be built on dialogue, not rhetoric. But Huck was overshadowed by a new breed of fakestyle jolly giants—reckless, ruthless, chauvinistic. Horatio Greenough was wrong when he complained that America has "no half-fabulous, legendary wealth, no misty, cloud-enveloped background." A more accurate diagnosis might be that America deliberately rejected these elements of her past in order to create a new interpretation of history.

The Greeks used mythological metaphors as the basis for heroic style; the Romans depended on biographical archetypes; the Middle Ages on hagiography. By stressing a few themes and patterns each epoch greatly increased the focus and intensity of meaning. There is no such cohesive force in American culture—hence no such clarity or intensity. We may get it, for the first time, in the new pop iconography.

Meanwhile, we struggle with the aesthetics and heroics of impermanence. To modern critics an art-object is a temporary center of energy, which motivates for a while, then dies. America went into a furor in 1913 over Marcel Duchamp's "Nude Descending a Staircase." Half a century later—as Duchamp himself admitted—the Nude was dead; she had become a tombstone to her still-living creator. The same can be said about heroic acts, such as Lindbergh's 1927 solo crossing of the Atlantic. Today impermanence is not only an observable fact, but a stylistic device.[8]

Another key word is *interface*. Originally a chemical term referring to the interaction of substances in a kind of mutual irritation, it has been broadened to deal with the whole culture. In its most natural form interface emerges as random conversation or dialogue—bits and snatches. This is what we see on the avant-garde stage. The interplay of multiple aspects generates insights and discovery. Interface is random contact with the life of forms. One by-product is a new heroic style. The hero becomes a happening. Whatever happens, this style will not be simple or linear. To be contemporary is to give up simple explanations of man and his world, to embrace complexity once and for all, to try both to manage and image it.

Heroic deeds are generally done in mysterious places, where obstacles are as great as imagination unencumbered by fact can make them. This described the Holy Land in the thirteenth century, the brave new world in the seventeenth, the American frontier in the nineteenth. Today, mystery dwells in outer space and on other planets. *What is it like out there?* Will those who go "out there" ever tell us? Perhaps the reign of words will come to an end, along with man's bondage to gravity. Scientists already do things that cannot be made intelligible in words, only in formulae. We may be abolishing speech as the most vital communication between men. This implies that the life of action, the matching of great words with great deeds, might end.

To continue with space-age metaphors, we are all crew members on a single global spaceship, making our way through infinity. The voyage our earth makes is precarious. We depend on a thin layer of atmosphere above us, and a hero at the helm—these, and nothing more.

If we are to survive, we must know the other crewmen, even if we don't like them. Entering the final quarter of the twentieth century, we must invent new systems, symbols, and rituals. They must be born out of processes in which we participate, but over which we have no conscious control.

Western man lives in a society where most old myths have lost their mana and power. He no longer accepts either the motifs or the materials of Christian mythos, which served him well for centuries. His has been that most terrible of fates—he is demythologized.

When an old mythology disintegrates, a new one originates. To survive is to remythologize. Instead of *discovering* a new mythos, we find ourselves *participating* in it. That is what our pop artists and pop heroes are doing, what our children are seeking with their new tactics, songs, morals, haircuts. They will bury not only us, but our worn-out mythology, too.

When Western demythologizing reached its crest, between the World Wars, a doom boom resulted. Darkness, despair, and doubt spread everywhere. *The Waste Land* that T. S. Eliot described in his 1922 poem was bone-dry:

> He who was living is now dead
> We who were living are now dying
> With a little patience
> Here is no water but only rock
> Rock and no water but only rock.[9]

No place for the hero to thrive here. Other things withered, too—laissez-faire economics, Newtonian physics, stiff-collar diplomacy. The "modern" world, as that term was understood by Locke, Jefferson, Voltaire, and Gladstone, gave way to a post-modern world. Inevitably the heroic style changed radically. The arts pointed the way. Daniel French gave way to Alexander Calder, John Singer Sargent to Jackson Pollock, Stephen Foster to Dizzie Gillespie. We left the world of Descartes and Newton, with closed boxes, for that of Einstein and Wernher von Braun, with infinitely open spaces. The structure of society, the order of ideas, the basic concepts of space and time were up-ended. Where there had been time-honored myth suddenly there was a void. Even the existence of God, that hero of heroes, was questioned. The church found itself in the embarrassing position of having within its affluent confines everything it needed—except God.

One of the brightest popstyle theologians, Harvey Cox, urges his fellow churchmen to seek God not in the sacred cloister, but in the secular city. How, he asks, can man separate sacred and secular, when they are both God's? The sacred always goes bad unless it is working with the secular; the word becomes mere vapor unless it becomes flesh. There is no theology without sociology. No matter how pure and ethereal a religion may be at first, it is always converted into something else.

Realizing this, a group of tough-minded thinkers called existentialists have forced us to think about ultimate problems. Are we free? Have we ever been free? What does it mean to exist now, genuinely?

The golden thread of thought goes back to Plato, who pondered essences, and Aristotle, who stressed existence. That to him was reality. Man is as he does; action justifies life. Existence is action and involvement. In today's idiom—are you turned on?

Pop culture, with all its fadish stunts, asks these same questions in a new idiom. New sounds and stagings penetrate the modern conditions, ridiculing outworn dogmas and platitudes. There are many different ways and levels on which existential concern can be shown. Our cultural package is all of a piece. Change seems most radical in some areas only because we know more about them, or are more involved with them. The radical common denominator is that we accept change as a normal condition. *Dubito, ergo sum.*

Lest we get bogged down in generalities, and Cartesian parodies, we might profit from seeing precisely how a standard "fakestyle hero" —the old-time detective—becomes "popstyle" as the new super-spy. The detective, alias the Private Eye, is essentially the cowboy in from the open plains to tackle the closed confusion of Big Town. He is still a wanderer, and a gentleman; resigned to a violence he cannot escape, determined to "do what he has to do" . . . not a romantic lover, but good gonads . . . not seducing but seduced. The direct representative of the gods (before he passed on to Valhalla in 1972, some would have said of J. Edgar Hoover), the Private Eye was a sort of temple prostitute, propitiating fate by sexual means and a gun that passed easily for a phallic symbol.

Reduced to a pulp by Mike's hammer, the Private Eye became after World War II the Super Spy. He was bonded, numbered, sent out on missions impossible. Like his animal compatriots, Mickey Mouse and Batman, he is immortal—even as he upends the old detective formulae:

Detective (fakestyle)	Super-Spy (popstyle)
Unilinear	Multi-linear
Regional	International
Detects	Projects

A loner	Team man
Fights a man	Fights an ideology
Moral	Amoral
Job-oriented	Role-oriented

From Descartes through Hegel, Western thought was dominated by rationalism, system-building, and the notion of progress. As in formal theology, house-wrecking has been the order of the day. Dominant themes of twentieth-century philosophy are disillusionment, pessimism, the lure of destruction. Paradox prevails; we live at a moment of economic optimism, and political pessimism. Automation, computerization, nuclear fission, and rocketry should have made us free—but have only tyrannized us to a degree unparalleled in history. Our ancestors thought we would, by now, have built the brave new world. Instead, we seem unable to prevent blowing it up. Here is the overwhelming problem for contemporary heroes to face and solve.

They must learn to cross new bridges, touch new godheads. Think how theology could be enriched by encompassing ecology, which studies the inter-relationship of organisms and their environment. Until recently, ecology was largely the bailiwick of biologists concentrating on plant environments. Now ecologists say man's total environment includes not only the physical and biotic, but the cultural and conceptual. Material from the traditional humanities, arts, social sciences—and why not theology?—should be gathered. Only inter-disciplinary efforts can focus on the holistic man in his total surroundings. Man is moving into an era of *total environment* and radical new styles. Confronted with that movement, theologians would seem to have three alternatives—change the image they now present, adapt to needs of twentieth-century society, or retreat into pedantic triviality.

If only yesterday's heroes and saints are revered, in the capitol and the cathedral, the government and church will emerge as the safe-deposit box where archaic images are stored. To find new heroes, institutions must make adjustments. In rethinking they may see that new ideas and labels apply admirably to old truths. Christianity as revealed through the Gospels is a kind of happening. Why should He have been conceived of a Virgin, rejected by His own people, hung on a cross? Was ever a story more astounding (to the unbeliever, absurd) than this? While oldstyle theologians mourn the death of

God, new media let their light shine on all men. The shining light—
epiphany! God is dead only for those who seek Him in a square
tomb. He's definitely alive for those watching the tube.

To recognize the absence of myth is the first step toward resur-
recting it. By 1960, that recognition was widespread in America.
The heroic style is being refashioned. Remythologizing is under way.

America has never been an aristocratic society, but it has aped
Europe's for generations. If America was (to quote Mark Twain)
"fresh out of kings," it produced scores of kings and queens for
sports events, agricultural fairs, and every product on the store shelf.
In our ambivalent effort to establish democracy, we first concentrated
on politics (during our Revolution), then economics (during the New
Deal). Perhaps we can now create an environmental democracy, in
which we both accept and improve the twentieth-century world.
The March of the Poor on Washington in 1968 showed how far we
still have to go. We must not be afraid of America, the things in it,
the way it operates. Boredom, frustration, repetition, waste, and
delay are all built into the model. A new generation no longer thinks
of used-car lots, billboards, and flashing neon signs as part of the
Wasteland. Instead they are raw material for visual involvement—
the stuff out of which pop heroes are made. The entire environment
can be seen as a work of art, a teaching machine designed to maxi-
mize perception. For the first time artists can be, in the full sense
of the word, popular heroes. But it must be on the people's terms,
not the elite's.

When most men lived in the country, folkstyle allowed us to
mythologize American culture. By deflating rural values, fakestyle
demythologized our lives. The job today is to remythologize them.

Certain distinctions between the main heroic styles in the last
three centuries emerge not as factual syllogisms, but as suggestions.

Folkstyle	Fakestyle	Popstyle
oral	verbal	multisensory
traditional	nostalgic	experimental
realistic	romantic	psychedelic
earthy	sticky	tart
homespun	factory-spun	polyester
continuity	transition	explosion
improvised	ersatz	electronic
cowboy	Buffalo Bill	Bonanzaland
community sing	folk festival	Disneyland

Stylistic changes are reflected in the work of young writers like Susan Sontag and Tom Wolfe, young campus heroes like David Harris. In *Against Interpretation* Miss Sontag includes an essay "On style," arguing that style is the principle of decision in a work of art, the signature of the artist's will. She puts her own signature on "Notes on Camp," widely regarded as one of the most influential essays of the decade. "Camp" is love of the unnatural—of artifice and exaggeration. She traces camp's origins to eighteenth-century Gothic novels, chinoiserie, and artificial ruins, and sees it responding to "instant character," thus supplementing the new Age of Circuitry. New style-makers are usually not writers, according to Miss Sontag, but artists, film-makers, social planners, TV technicians, neurologists, electronics engineers, and sociologists. Basic texts for this new cultural alignment are found in the writings of Marshall McLuhan, Buckminster Fuller, John Cage, Siegfried Gidieon, Norman O. Brown, and Gyorgy Kepes. "Sensations, feelings, the abstract forms and styles of sensibility count. It is to these that contemporary art addresses itself."[10] The way of camp is not in terms of beauty, but of stylization. Are we to witness the rise of campstyle in America?

If so, Tom Wolfe must be accounted a Daniel Boone who led us across its frontier. Touring the country to find out about postwar teen-age culture, Wolfe chose the name for his full-length report from the incredibly stylized custom cars California kids design and produce —*Kandy-Kolored Tangerine-Flake Streamline Baby*. In the "Introduction" style is central to his whole thesis:

> Since World War II classes of people whose styles of life had
> been practically invisible had the money to build monuments
> to their own styles. This took the form of custom cars, the
> twist, the jerk, the monkey, the shake, rock music generally,
> stretch pants, decal eyes. All these things, like Inigo Jones's
> classicism, have started having an influence on the life of the
> whole country.

To Wolfe, Baby Jane Holzer, the society girl who went pop, is "the hyperversion of a whole new style of life in America." She is a symbol, just as is Las Vegas—"the Versailles of America, the only architecturally uniform city in the Western World." Gangsters built it in an isolated spot, just as Louis XIV went outside Paris to create his fantastic baroque environment. The Las Vegas hoods celebrated, very early, the new style of life of America—"using the money pumped in by the war to show a prose vision of style."

Wolfe's special hero—"The Last American Hero"—is Junior Johnson, the Carolina country boy who learned to drive by running whisky for his bootlegging father and grew up to be a famous stock-car racing driver. "Junior Johnson is one of the last of those sports stars who is not just an ace at the game itself, but a hero a whole people or class of people can identify with."[11] He "turns on" the white Southerner the way Jack Dempsey stirred up the Irish and Joe Louis the Negroes. Johnson is a modern popstyle hero, involved with car culture and car symbolism; Wolfe is his Boswell.

His images are as hard-edged, clear, objective, precise as pop painting, or as the two-minute summaries by a master popstyle TV journalist like Eric Sevareid. Here is Wolfe's description of the IRT subway station at 50th and Broadway at 8:45 on a Thursday morning:

> All the faces come popping in clots out of the Seventh Avenue local, past the King Size Ice Cream machine, and the turnstiles start whacking away as if the world were breaking up on the reefs. Four steps past the turnstiles everybody is already backed up haunch to paunch for the climb up the ramp and the stairs to the surface, a great funnel of flesh, wool, felt, leather, rubber and steaming alumicron, with the blood squeezing through everybody's old sclerotic arteries in hopped-up spurts from too much coffee and the effort of surfacing from the subway at the rush hour.

The tendency here, and in most pop prose, is not to pontificate, but to probe, to twist the cultural kaleidoscope, to travel without a road map. And that, you may be sure, the Old Boys can never approve. No wonder they have trouble with Barbara Garson's *MacBird!* This gay, gaudy play, most widely heralded political parody in the 1960s, goes its own outrageous way, toward no particular point. MacBird's outcry sums it up: "Unity, Unity, wherefore art thou, Unity?" Lyndon B. Johnson has the distinction of being the first presidential anti-hero in American history. Other presidents (including an earlier Johnson) have been attacked and scorned, but only popstyle could have done it in this manner.

Once the beatnik witches have assured Johnson (alias MacBird) that he can be president if Kennedy (alias John Ken O'Dunc) is assassinated, our shotgun parody is off and popping. The Egg of Head (Adlai Stevenson), the Earl of Warren, the Wayne of Morse, and Lord McNamara get into the act. Everyone does his thing. Riots, sit-ins, foreign interventions, demonstrations, and skullduggery play their part in the creation of a new Pox Americana. In the words of MacBird:

> We mean to be the firemen of peace
> Dousing flames with freedom's forceful flow.

Paradoxically, the mediocrity of the play serves a purpose. The more it puts us on, the clearer becomes the message. What can you do with a parody that parodies straw men and falsehoods rather than real men and foibles? Will the real catharsis please stand up?

MacBird is a minor play pointing to a major tendency—to ridicule not only people, but art-forms. The line between "impure life" and "pure art" is no longer considered valid. Not only Happenings but public events and demonstrations become theater. In a real sense, the various riots, marches, and protests of the 1960s were means for dramatic expression and catharsis in American life. The TV screen became Everyman's theater. Everyone had a box seat.

In this setting no one can *plan* to be a hero, the way a general plans a battle or an architect a building. No one knows when he is "on stage" or "off stage"—which camera is focusing on which person now? (No wonder President Nixon avoided campaign television debates.) Or, if there are six cameras, which button is the studio technician pushing to put one image into 100,000,000 minds, and keep the other five out? If we leave mass media, do we move *into* the action or *away* from it?

Such questions open up the whole area of leisure in popstyle America. Just what we can anticipate is explored in the Spring 1968 issue of *TDR, The Drama Review*. The day of Fun Palace is upon us, where Gala Days and Nights will be filled with:

Instant Cinema	Juke Box Information
Genius Chat	Adult Toys
Clownery	Star Gazing
Fireworks	Concerts
Battles of Flowers	Rallies
Science Gadgetry	Learning Machines
Kunst Dabbling	Theater

All for your delight! New wealth, mobility, flexibility, and social interdependence demand an awareness of the vast range of influences and experiences open to all at all times. Since the Fun Palace Foundation was registered as a Charitable Trust, some of these dreams-on-paper may be realities within a few years.[12]

Already the reach is on for new modes of expression; new discoveries are on display. Thus, a single issue of the avantgarde popstyle newspaper *Village Voice*, advertises:

"The Space Music of Sun Ra"—A Freeform Excursion into the Far
   Reaches of Sound and Sight
"Alive, Through the Glass Lightly"—A Turn on For Kids and Adults
   Who Never Believed Alice Was 9 Feet High
"Hair—The American Tribal Love-Rock Musical."

Ads such as these, plus the staccato prose of Stephanie Harrington, Leticia Kent, Don McNeill, Michael McDonald, and Sally Kempton, made the *Village Voice* one of the best barometers of style-change, and proof that sensitive reporting comes in any style, any idiom.

They also suggest that in their newstyle involvement with popular culture, young Americans are discovering new modes of experiences, new ways to achieve depth and total involvement. Old walls of snobbery and elitism are tumbling down. The "highbrow" seems more and more ridiculous as he preens his own feathers. In an incredibly varied and altering culture, we find a priceless artistic and stylistic pluralism. If we can separate the real from the phony, the serious from the pseudo, we may move into one of man's most creative epochs. This calls for skillful and interdisciplinary criticism, which will "both confront the implications of the new sensibility and build on the substantial achievements of the mass culture critics."[13] This is indeed a major responsibility of the new intellectual generation.

Recent activities within the historian's camp indicate that this confrontation is taking place. The "consensus school" of the 1950s, which held that most of the heated controversies of America's past were hyperbolic, a kind of ritual warfare associated with politics, has been challenged and in some instances discredited.[14] America is not "one nation under God, indivisible." Tension, not consensus, is the dominating theme. A "New Left" school of radical historians will have nothing to do with consensus and the Establishment. Chief among their heroes is Herbert Marcuse, who calls for intolerance against movements from the right and toleration of movements from the left— since the left alone is the agent of history. To avoid the "systematic moronization" of America we must resist goods and services that render us incapable of achieving an existence of our own and make us "one dimensional men." Living in what another able young historian, Michael Harrington, calls *The Accidental Century*, we must move *Toward a Democratic Left.* We must have more democratic debate and more effective popular control over huge government programs if our democracy is to endure, he argues. One hears the echoes of the old Jeffersonian line: "Give the people light and they will find their way."

As the writings of men like Harrington show, the fear of apathy and automation that saturated the 1950's has changed to violence and the fear of revolution in the 1970's. Students, linked together as never before in the Age of Circuitry, are revolting everywhere. No more talk of the "Silent Generation." Obviously young people are turned on— engaged in an intense search for personal commitment. Seeking a prototype, Gina Berriault chose David Harris, 1967 student president at Stanford University.[15] Harris has pale-blue eyes, rimless glasses, a substantial mustache that makes him appear older than twenty-one, and large photoes of Charlie Chaplin and Mahatma Gandhi on his wall. The books on his shelf are Nietzsche, Kierkegaard, A. J. Muste, and the *Upanishad.* He talks with a fast mixture of beat jargon, academic terms, and words in common usage. Meeting for the first time with Stanford's President Wallace Sterling, Harris wore a work shirt, Levis, and moccasins. He doesn't dress oldstyle, one presumes, because he doesn't think oldstyle; in the words of Thoreau (a popstyle favorite), he listens to the music of a different drummer.

So do his contemporaries whose student lectures were published under the title *A Student Look at America* (1967). One of them, twenty-five-year-old Louis Cartwright, said that the new hero is one who "knows nobody knows—and isn't afraid of not knowing." The key to the heroic personality is not achievement, but potential, since "we are a potential world of men who require no corrals." The New Reality, says twenty-eight-year-old Phil Baumgartner, is "the power of courage to bring the individual so immediately in contact with the here-and-now that all expectation or possibility of death is wiped out."[16]

All around us we see the "failure of success." Studies of alienated youth who will make and be tomorrow's heroes indicate they will not settle for the bag of toys that fasincated devotees of Horatio Alger. Typical of the times was Jan Myrdal's *Confessions of a Disloyal European.* Son of the great Swedish economist whose book *An American Dilemma: The Negro Problem and Modern Democracy* helped shape a whole generation of liberal thinking, Jan sings not a hymn, but a eulogy to revolution. Our civilization is full of promises that are never fulfilled—reeking with bad faith. Prejudice and hatred are wrong, war is madness, massive inequality is intolerable. Suddenly the world seems filled with young people who are neither ideologues nor psychological misfits, but pragmatists who had no recourse but to become radicals. Not only their politics but their programs are radical. There is no vaccination against the "malaise of affluence." Thus Jan Myrdal describes himself lying in a bed he has not made or left for three weeks, practicing yoga breathing with his legs up against the wall.[17] Young people around the world seem on the same wavelength. What does this imply for the hero, American style?

Young men and women who formulate this lifestyle reflect the mood of the 1970's. They also remind us, after our survey of several centuries, that man is the only being who asks questions about being —about power and potential beyond himself. Power plus structure equals a life of being. America is searching for a new ontology. Cultural relocation and heroic transformation are radical interests of a new generation.

Image-makers are engaged in a worldwide scavenger hunt involving African sculpture, Zen fables, Indian music, the camp style of Victoria, the click-clack of computers, the primitive masks of Mali. By telescoping time, tradition, and geography the first universal heroic tradition may emerge. All world history is its past; all the world's its stage. The arts may be one before the church is one. The atelier is more ecumenical than the altar.

Yet it is not in the church but in the laboratory that the germs of this culture will best flourish. Science is the foundation of the new mythos. There are indications that biology may be grasping the lead from physics. The whole psychedelic spectrum, like work with DNA and RNA, points to revolutionary ideas. They will be dramatized in new heroes. We are on the verge of what the twentieth century's greatest poet, William Butler Yeats, called *The Second Coming:*

> The darkness drops again; but now I know
> That twenty centuries of stony sleep
> Were vexed to nightmare by a rocking cradle,
> And what rough beast, its hour come round at last,
> Slouches toward Bethlehem to be born?[18]

NOTES

[1]Thomas Hall, *The Loathesomeness of Long Hair . . . With an Appendix Against Painting, Spots, Naked Breasts, Etc.* (London, 1654).

[2]Ihab Hassan, *Radical Innocence: Studies in the Contemporary American Novel* (New York: Harper and Row, 1961), p. 6.

[3]Thomas C. Cochran, "The History of a Business Society," *Journal of American History*, LIV (June, 1967), 9.

[4]The Archives of American Folk Song in the Library of Congress has more than 40,000 pieces of recorded folk music; there are thousands more in state and regional archives, as well as regular commercial issues. In *Folksongs on Records* (1950), Ben Gray Lumpkins lists over 4,000 titles.

[5]"Irving pretended both childishness and antiquity for America, then stood back and saw these things fail before an always triumphant broad daylight which existed to celebrate the absence of childishness and antiquity," writes Terence Martin in "Rip, Ichabod, and the American Imagination," *American Literature*, XXI (May, 1959), 148.

[6]John A. Kouwenhoven, *The Arts in Modern American Civilization* (New York: Norton, 1967), p. 89. Kouwenhoven's analysis of "bric-a-brac" America provides a good introduction to the subject of fakestyle.

[7]Quoted by John Kouwenhoven, *Made in America* (New York: Norton, 1960), p. 89; reprinted as *Arts in Modern American Civilization* (New York: Norton, 1967).

[8]Harold Rosenberg explores this subject in *The Anxious Object* (New York: Horizon, 1965).

[9]Excerpt from "The Waste Land" by T. S. Eliot. Reprinted by permission of the publishers, Harcourt Brace Jovanovich, Inc.

[10]Susan Sontag, *Against Interpretation* (New York: Dell, 1967), p. 300.

[11]Tom Wolfe, *The Kandy-Kolored Tangerine-Flake Streamline Baby* (New York: Farrar, Straus, 1965), p. 131 (paperback ed., Pocket Books, 1967).

[12]Preliminary drawings and a "Non-Program" for a Laboratory of Fun appear in *TDR, The Drama REview*, T XXXIX (Spring, 1968), 127 ff.

[13]John G. Cawelti, "Reviews," *American Quarterly*, XX (September, 1968), 259.

[14]See John A. Garraty, "A Then for Now," *The New York Times* (May 12, 1967), Section 7, p. 1.

[15]Gina Berriault, "The New Student President, David Harris of Stanford," *Esquire*, September, 1967.

[16]Otto Butz, ed., *To Make a Difference* (New York: Harper & Row, 1967), p. 231.

[17]Jan Myrdal, *Confessions of a Disloyal European* (New York: Pantheon, 1968). See also Kenneth Keniston, *Young Radicals: Notes on Committed Youth* (New York: Harcourt, Brace, Jovanovich, 1968).

[18]From "The Second Coming," *Collected Poems* by William Butler Yeats. Copyright 1924 by The Macmillan Company, renewed 1952 by Bertha Georgie Yeats. Reprinted by permission of The Macmillan Company.

By FRED MacFADDEN
The Pop Pantheon

Popular religion in the Western world may be said to be of two kinds—religious, chiefly Christian, and political, chiefly democratic. Hence, before our very eyes, we have seen Pogo boosted for President of the U.S., and Snoopy touted as the type of Christ. A very likely Vice-Presidential candidate to run with Pogo would be Diana Prince (Wonder Woman), who would secretly be known as Madame President. As for Snoopy, his John the Baptist would have to be that eater of the new new communion, Tiny Tim, whose religious ecstasies are brought on by the consumption of a dish of pudding while in a state of seclusion.

There can be no doubt that the characters named above have charisma. Charisma is Admiral George Dewey passing under a triumphal arch of lath, plaster, and wood. But then Admiral George Dewey lost his charisma, and his triumphal arch, instead of being converted to marble, was allowed to wither away, a comic strip travesty (after all, lathes are wood, wood gives paper, and paper gives comic strips). A living comic strip was Teddy Roosevelt's mug. His face was so flexible and expressive, says Dixon Wecter, that his face was the answer to a cartoonist's prayer. Furthermore, in the eyes of some shrewd observers, T. R. never got past the age of six. Yet here was a face carved heroically on Mt. Rushmore along with Washington,

27

Jefferson, and Lincoln. T. R., we would say, bodes well for the great religion-to-be of democratic humor.

I wouldn't be surprised one day to pass a church with a stained glass window showing Superman in full flight. After all, isn't Clara Barton eulogized in a stained-glass window in the Winchester, Mass., Unitarian Church, as well as, more strangely, in a stained-glass panel in St. Thomas' Episcopal Church, on Fifth Avenue, in New York City? In many ways she was a superwoman. Why not the same honor to Superman? Well, but you say, Superman was first published in the spring of 1939, according to Stephen Becker. He even beat out Hitler's march into Poland and was obviously an American rival to the mythic hero developed by Carlyle, Nietzsche, Schicklgruber, *et Cie*? Furthermore, you say, what about thirteen-year-old Pyong-sop Chong, a Seoul schoolboy, who recently hanged himself trying to imitate his favorite cartoon hero, able to die and bring himself back to life at will? What about the child who said, "Superman is bad because they make him sort of a God."[1] What about Charles Johnson, who back a while ago said, "I am going to join Abe Lincoln," after the President's assassination, and so cut his throat, according to Wecter? Doesn't hero-worship have bad seeds in it? Look how first baseman Eddie Waitkus was shot by Ruth Ann Steinhagen, with her "Herostratus complex." And look how miserable Lindbergh's life was made as he was buffeted, like a fetish, between the love and hate of the American public.

Well, Jules Feiffer to our rescue! Jules reinforces Milton's *Aeropagitica.* We must run the risk of hanging ourselves or worshipping brutality because we must investigate our innermost being through the study of literature, including comic books. The repressions and inhibitions of life must be teased by fantasy in our youth, given an escape valve (and when do we leave off being juveniles?). We must believe in Samson Shillitoe, who comes back stronger than ever, completely impervious to a pre-frontal lobotomy, in *A Fine Madness,* a 1966 film. In a *Big Valley* episode, Barbara Stanwyk comes through absolutely unruffled, completely unscathed, after enduring the most fiendish tortures at the hands of an arch monster. And we are glad!

Wecter tells us that in the early days of Soviet collectivization, photographs of Henry Ford and Lenin replaced the icons of the Holy Family and St. Basil in the households of some peasants! We're not

sure about Lenin, but have you ever looked at photographs of Henry
Ford—*the* Henry Ford? A surge of awed laughter convulses the pit of
the stomach as we stare into his fierce-eyed mug. If there is more
room on Mt. Rushmore, put Ford next to T. R.! Said Chauncey
Depew, "After seventy years of political experience I can't understand
the psychology which makes Ford a presidential candidate."[2] But as
Wecter points out, American heroes are different from European
heroes. The birthday of an American hero is celebrated like a saint's
day. An American hero or heroine is not a person but an institution.
Yet our strong types can also be caricatured, like Lincoln, like T. R.
Caricature can also be unconscious, as when a George Washington is
apotheosized or a Ben Franklin turned into a magician. This is a result
of our Puritan democratic heritage, which reaches back even to the
Byzantine iconoclasts who daubed the faces of Christ with whitewash,
and to the nomadic Israelites as they emerged into a monotheistic
stance. Was there not a charismatic love that emanated from the
cartoon icons of FDR? And what were his relics which we could
"mix" with our colored inks? Memories of fireside chats? Eleanor
carrying a pistol on her at all times for fear he would get her? Putting
it all together, and adding the fact that the Edison-Ford-Tom-Swift
inventor hero had started us on a Lindy Hop towards the year 2001
A.D., it is not surprising at all that Henry Ford should have that
religio-democratic charisma which would entitle him to a transfer of
the mantle of worship from the shoulders of Thomas Edison. The
same applied to FDR and his "Federal god," Jefferson; to Lee and
Lincoln's inspiration, Washington; and to the musical charisma played
off between Al Capp's Kigmy and Snoopy.

If Europeans would search their literary traditions, they would
find rousing comic book episodes. What about *The Big Dip,* starring
Beowulf and Unferth? Beowulf: Hwaet! List to my lay of the beasts
of the whale road, the murderous deeps, my furious struggles. Unferth:
!x!#&XX!!! Or how about Enkidu, Gilgamesh's partner, being
tamed by a temple prostitute, for an example from Mesopotamia?
Enkidu: What are you? Tarara: List to my lay. . . . Or, for a serious
comic book episode, what Christ dressed up as the "king" that he
secretly is, in the praetorium, after the Roman soldiers have scourged
him, would remind you of another meek, incognito superman, Clark
Kent, able to leap tall buildings at a single bound? The horrors of
suffering don't make any difference. The enemy is defeated, for the

Christ has an army of angels at his beck and call. He can afford to don the cartoon garishness of purple robe, iron "sceptre," and thorny crown, even as Superman can afford to don glasses and acne. For behind the ridiculous facade lurks tempestuous unlimited power bursting at the seams. What an improvement in charisma over Moses, who is frequently seen as Jesus' charismatic forebear. Moses stretches huge and lofty as Michelangelo's statue. It is difficult to find any funnies in his anecdotes. But what about the many panels and strips by which Jesus makes gentle mockery of exaltation, both Roman and Jewish style—the story of the tribute money in the fish's mouth, for example, and for another, the tale of sawed-off Zacchaeus, the hated tax-collector (played by Mickey Rooney), who promised Christ that he would give half his goods to the poor and make up for any fraudulence fourfold, thus elevating himself above the self-importance of his fellow Jews and bringing this day salvation to his house. Or how about the Lamont Cranston bit, as Jesus disappears in the midst of those who would throw him off the cliff. Some capers for Lord Buckley's "Naz," the "carpenter kitty," what? Could anything good come out of Nazareth? Betcha!

The rhetorical preachment was asked by Peter Cartwright, "Where is the man who, like the primitive Christian, walks toward heaven barefoot and clad in sackcloth?" At this, Johnny Appleseed arose, barefoot, dressed in raggedy trousers, a shirt made out of coffee sacking with holes cut in it for his arms and neck, and with a tin mush pan for a hat, and said, "Here is your primitive Christian." Do we need to go into all the monuments erected to Johnny and his place in our folk literature, to convince ourselves that he belongs in the pop pantheon? Similarly, need we argue too strenuously for Pat Paulsen, one of the living panel figures, as a minor deity, at least? At least 283 voters gave him the nod in the New Hampshire primaries, for a grand figure of about one per cent. This wouldn't touch the "Apotheosis of Washington," a huge painting placed in our National Capitol, nor the much touted chintz of Washington and Franklin showing the General with the goddess of independence riding in a chariot drawn by leopards. And Paulsen, being funny first and serious second, will probably never have a balloon prayer attached to his mouth such as was ascribed to young Georgie Washington by Morrison "Uncle Juvinell" Heady: "Good Santa Claus, be kind to me while I am sleeping peacefully."[3]

We say this or that person is "colorful." Does color have charisma?

MacDougall says that the first colored comic was circulated in the U.S. on Sunday, Nov. 18, 1894, in the *NY World.* It was a six-box by F. Outcault called the "Origin of the Species."[4] Well, Sunday seemed the "natural day" to use color, which was expensive but which would up sales, Hearst felt.[5] Color was a novelty. Feiffer says the *World-Telegram* for a while "ran an anemic four-page color supplement" on Saturday. "An embarrassing day for color supplements. They so obviously belonged to Sunday."[6] Why? In Feiffer's case, it probably was simply the day of leisure, when a kid would want to sprawl out, along with the rest of the family and plunge into the psychedelic medium, color comics, that expanded the mind like the first game of a doubleheader at the ball park on a Sunday, or the universal terror served up as a radio appetizer just before meal time along the twilight, soggy, grey eastern seaboard: the "Shadow," on the sabbath. But what does Robert Field mean that the Sunday comics were glorified with color, that it gave them "their final form"?[7] And beyond final form, color could lend scope and dimension, as in the work of George Herriman.[8] Surrealism, realism, and reality could become a powerful fact, through the image or icon at varying distance, whose position is brought out in contrasting color.

In the eye of man, color has magical charisma because it has reality. Lancelot Hogben speaks of the prehistoric paintings which were frequently colored the same shade as the deer and bison; which were depicted as some kind of charm for lucky hunting, he says.[9] The original idol of Pallas Athene seems to have had lots of vivid, radiant color on her shield and about her armor, and her eyes were of colored stone. She was the ancient counterpart of Hippolyta, Wonder Woman's mother, or she played herself, in the adventure strip of the Amazon warriors. Together they gave depth of miraculous tradition to Wonder Woman herself. The main vehicle for this magical feeling is color. Leroy Campbell, steeped in Mithraic lore, feels that the color red may mean "physical life or vitality," in the sacred cave paintings which have been the subject of his study for many years. Black may be "for death or materiality, purple for sovereign force, and yellow for generative heat. Gold is for sunlight or cosmic fire."[10] And so, as we peruse the latest issue of *Wonder Woman,* we reflect on her black hair and white costume in a contemporary story, and on her blue, red, and gold costume in a retrospective tale of her girlhood.[11] Light and its absence, light and its primary compo-

nents: we have here a scientific lesson, we have an entertaining reminder of our own colorful depth perceptions, but we have something
more. It is the magical power to obtain the reality which we desire,
from which we draw the spiritual stuff that our ancestors found in
the nutritious blood and flesh of the deer and bison.

Charisma is perhaps the mortar that binds the icon, the fastness
that splits the light on the cartoon panel and defines the light-filled
portions as well. Rosy Bonheur's oil prints of Buffalo Bill maintain
the spirit of the original worship long after the man has fallen into
"sham hero-worship," as Bill put it, according to Wecter. Similarly,
the iconography of Christ, first as boy shepherd, then as law-giver
and judge, trace down to the cartoon stills of *Jesus Christ Super-
star*, as ridiculous as Buffalo Bill printing the eye with a garish
panel as he races around exploding glass bubbles with a popgun that,
unbeknownst, fires scatter-shot so that he can't miss. The dawn of the
hero and heroine deepens into a rationalistic twilight. Wonder
Woman no longer flies through the air with the greatest of ease, but
must depend on yoga and karate to see her through. And much
thinking on the paradox of Kingdom versus carnage has produced
our confused Superstar.

But the fixing of fresh icons based on the old charismas is a
habit which the people and their artists never lose. We will again
have our Thomas Nast, whose cartoons Lincoln thought "have never
failed to arouse enthusiasm and patriotism," and we will have our new
Wonder Woman to sweep eighty per cent of the popularity votes, as
she did in the Forties.[12] Dr. Richard A. Long, Director of the Center
for African and African-American Studies, at Atlanta University,
speaking recently at Coppin State College about Marcus Garvey, a
figure who is gaining increased attention, pointed out a tableau
incident which, in the opinion of this writer, bids fair to elevate
Garvey to at least the level of a tutelary spirit, if not that of a patriarchal
god. We refer to his meeting with the Ku Klux Klan to determine what
their goals were. This meeting was looked upon with horror by
W. E. B. DuBois, but if we reckon rightly, it is Garvey, not DuBois,
who will succeed with the people, because, in the spirit of the new
psychic and extrasensory charisma, he has no fear of the incongruous
to determine the nature of the vibrations. If pop charisma is humorous,
it may be because it is finally surfacing after lying latent in the great
traditions and writings of the ancient past.

The essence of modern charisma is that it produces kinetic icons. And this is particularly true in America. Wecter says, "America is the only country in the world which pretends to listen to the teaching of its founders as if they were still alive."[13] Traditionally, American scions have looked up to the practical vocations, while Germans and British have leaned toward the careers of their military heroes. This means that when a European, a Frenchman, for example, quotes Napoleon, there is a belletristic fineness in the scripture: "The bullet that will kill me is not yet cast." Or consider the grand way in which Napoleon spoke of himself as an event. But what do we have from Henry Ford? "History is bunk." And there is Edison, who had no rules around his shop, because, hell, they were trying to accomplish something around there. Such is the tenor of the religio-democratic gospel.

And for its paraphernalia, we have many fine icons to choose from. We have Robert Watts' "Hot Dogs" (1964), chrome-plated lead hot dogs fixed in a burnished collection plate.[14] We have the new flag shown on the eight-cent Peace Corps stamp, where some of the star spangles turn into doves and fly off the blue field (!). And, for pop pantheon museum, we have such items as cigar labels with the mugs of T. R., Judge Taft, et. al., colorfully portrayed. The Europeans have their matter of Rome, of France, and of Britain. But Americans have matter of Pop. The Emperor of China, with his three tiered altar, will have nothing on us.

But in what sense, exactly, have the Sixties and Seventies *widened* the credibility gap between the would-be hero of flesh and blood and his potential constituents, at the same time that they have *intensified* the amount of charisma (literally "yearning") which titillates, as it always has, the desire to succeed? The answer seems to be that charisma has been progressively internalized. Both leader and follower, under the influences of democratic socialization, privatism, and aversion to man-made mechanisms, have projected *themselves* in the stance, speech, and even superhero costume, as we shall see. We need to up-date Wecter, but not so as to completely turn around everything he says. With Daniel Boorstin, in *America and The Image of Europe,* we need to see the United States as *too* knowledgeable of its origins, whereas Europe was able, like all other world cultures, outside the U.S., to create a mythology where origins simply faded into an obscure past. But as the credibility gap widens, particularly

after the Berkeley uprising, an American mythology in fact is sub-
stantiated, and political leaders, as in France, for example, up to
DeGaulle, may be falsely cheered by their tinny-throated handfuls
and raspberried by their potential followers in this country, even as
their European counterparts were caricatured on idealistic grounds
of gainsaying the myth of national supremacy, during the eighteenth
and nineteenth centuries. Those earlier states were so productive of
credibility gaps that the internalization process brought forth at least
one example of the early crop of "jolly giants," to use Marshall
Fishwick's phrase—Charles DeGaulle, with his vision of a French-
unified Europe. Stepping ashore in England not many years before
his death, DeGaulle compared himself to Joan of Arc! It was remarked at the time that the French people knew what he meant by
that statement. Not similarly, but with humorous good omen for
the future, one tv commentator during the recent New Hampshire
primary, said that Muskie *looked* like Lincoln. The other tv commentator laughed at this, and, of course, as with the French, but
with a difference, all America could appreciate the side remarks.

We do indeed still attend to the words of our national heroes
as though they were alive, but, to qualify Wecter, we attend them
with risibilities at the ready. Behavior in the United States has finally
come so far wide of the mythological mark (with catalytic assist
from the probing eyes of the media) that in self-defense we are prepared to sing "hey lilly buleros" far transcending "American Pie."
Pressure of internalizing charisma is mounting. What McLuhan takes
for mere costume partying in the global theatre is, more profoundly,
donning Superman's cape, the Lone Ranger's mask, Captain America's
tights, and seven-league boots, to see who will be the first to find the
way to Wonder Woman's buried lassoo, the charismatic instrument
necessary to pull the people together. Everybody is hero. A state
college president cultivates Eleanor Roosevelt, hoping to snatch the
presidency of the United States! An undergraduate touts himself for
Mayor of Baltimore during the recent election. Even Pogo has a go
at the polls. Boorstin, writing in the Sixties, could not see that American visionary art was pointing toward a liberation from dependence
on the image of Europe. Such works as Steinbeck's *Burning Bright*,
T.S. Eliot's *Confidential Clerk*, J.D. Salinger's *Catcher In The Rye*, Saul Bel-
low's *Henderson The Rain King*, and Robert Penn Warren's *All The King's Men*

are the signal for a popular liberation from the cloak-and-dagger Machiavel-
lianism of Europe. But, as Michael Brunson, a student of Captain
America, has pointed out to us, the campstyle return of the savior
of America, now projected as the big brother to the world, in con-
sonance with the earlier protagonists of our leading writers, reveals
the Fifties as a cooking period when other, cloak-and-fist, heroes,
such as Superman and Batman, would also return via advertising and
television, to tackle villains in the image of internal national stresses.
But the full cooking-up period would last through the Placid (or
Anxious?) Fifties.

It is probably true to say that most cartoon strips and animations
can be appreciated on at least three charismatic levels. For example,
even the phrase "dynamic duo," particularly referring to Batman and
Robin, can mean nostalgic childhood retrospect to the middle-aged,
or satirical peer competition to young adults and intellectuals and
"camp" comrades, or epic and victorious heroism to the very young.
It is with this last group that we must be chiefly concerned, for, if
another generation is not to lapse into the phases of skepticism and
regret, some measure must be taken of the virtual torrent of live and
animated funnies which have poured from keypunch to camera.
Socially directional material is one thing; mere escapist and Utopian
fare in the quantity now purveyed must beg the question, What *other*,
good human attributes, following the recent tv violence report (the
full one), if continuously bottled up in the unreal world of fantasy,
will, in contrast to the polarized world of actual behavior, cause even
worse social dislocations than are now being instigated in part by
documentary programs about real events? Further, we must, like good
science fiction thinkers, consider the possibility that the epic optimism
of the very young might just gather together to put into practice the
sayings of Spiderman and Batman—or that old hand-me-down, Superman's "truth, Justice, and the American way." Where would we be—
the Mad Hatters, Mysterios, and Dr. No's? Naked trespassers on the
Island of the Lords of the Flies, with nothing in our hands?

There seems to be a process whereby we move up to and usually
through the charismatic levels of epic, camp, and nostalgia. We seem
to start with color, as we have said. Color contains the potential for
all the various types of real perception through images or icons at
varying distances. Hence, color contains the potential for realized
unity with external objects of nature. A hero or heroine's essence

may be that color personality, expressed even to the cut and color of his costume, which makes him discrete, that is, finitely an individual. Here is a mirror universe, single as our own.

Seeing an individual stand out from the masses in our egocentric consciousness, we are immediately amused. The discreteness, the individuality of the costume before us—red-suited Buckingham Guard surplus with Captain Marvel medal, let us say (and nowadays, at least on college campuses, this is not an exaggeration)—possesses color in definition, and, by definition, possesses humor. This person really cuts a figure before us. And, to re-coin a phrase, if the colors in our eye be multiplied manifold, as indeed they are today, how great is that color!

It appears that we admire the humorous, if it etches on the retina of the eye a certain epic, camp, or nostalgic imprint. The sense of humor is at once a yearning, or charisma, which we experience when we perceive an object which we have not achieved and with which we do not have unity. Humor may be perception itself, the awareness of the unachieved, the irony of the unattainable at the moment.

The unachieved, in iconographic form, whether humanly or non-humanly geometric, is arranged through our mental processes into scaffoldings (such as symbolized by the scaffolding in the cartoonist Fellini's 8½), if we think in the abstract, or all the way to the end of the content development spectrum (such as in the film *Last Year At Marienbad,* whose creator, one of the "souls" of the comic strip-film liaison in France, has attempted to work with a "purified" charisma, one which consists of filming human silhouettes on bleached-out backgrounds, thus unifying color into a background of pure light). In *Last Year At Marienbad,* we are treated to a full pantheon of indoor and outdoor icons, heroic, chivalrous, and grand. They range from animal and human statuary to decor. The metaphysical juxtaposition of these images, the comic-strip "simultaneous" effects of the sequences, lend a tinge of humor, a magnetic draw, to the action. But since reality, as we have said, is generated by color, the final effect of "pure" iconography must be disappointing.

Reviewing a type of the charismatic process up to this point, we find color with definition has charisma for the state of perception; the response to charisma is an aspirational scaffolding or hierarchy (pantheon) of icons.

We now add that such iconification, or crystallizing out of a tropism toward discrete reality through the reflex of humorous perception, may take place with the result that icons become part of other icons or actually serve as starting points for other icons. An artistic sequence of icons may result, with a narrative beginning, middle, and end. A page of cartoon panels on a *Classic Comics* page illustrating the story of the thirty pieces of silver in the Gospels, could have such a sequentially charismatic effect, working as a magical charm through the presentation of color or reality to prompt a humorous, dramatic response. Similarly, if the eye proceeds up one side and down the other of an Andy Warhol pyramid of multi-colored Campbell soup cans, the result is basically the same, given a predisposition toward heroics, camp, or nostalgia, or any combination. The humor, or "humour," of the experience is fitted to the individual "hepness" out of which the respondent views the icon.

So that, given the vast evidence—ads, comic books, camp films, animation, tv commercials, etc.—it seems plain that the iconography of modern popular culture begins, as a perceptual experience, in the definition of color, that is to say reality itself, both with humorous potentialities and with humorous results. The image we seem to get of past centuries tells quite a different story, a story of communal rather than individual icon-pyramids, of austere upward worship rather than jovial at-ward worship. But of course, Harvey Cox's *Feast Of Fools* presents just that jovial side of the past which many of us have missed, and we will say a word more about his book later.

Wecter, then, is not wrong basically, when he says that our American "folk attitude toward our greatest heroes approaches the religious."[15] It is just that we have changed, possibly beginning with such expose biographers as Lytton Strachey, from a serious to a humorous stance toward our heroes. And if, as Pierre Couperie's fine study tells us, the comic strip "since birth has created the largest and most abundant iconographical field in history,"[16] then how much magnified must be the charismatic response, the humorous worship! For the charismatic process which we have been attempting to analyse is really a description of what we feel is the beginning and fulfillment of modern worship.

But we would quickly hasten to add that we would not want to confuse humorous worship with the new festal worship cum balloons which is being experimented with in some churches. We find disturbing the absence of *peccavis* of at least a modern sort in a recent Roman Catholic mass book. There is no humorous grotesquerie there to symbolize the real sins and spiritual disturbance in the midst of painful laughter, no more than there is in Episcopalian balloons. And to rebound *again,* we are not interested in *peccavi,* "I have sinned," from a traditionist viewpoint. We would turn the tessellations of the Man's jester hat in *Feast Of Fools* into thorn tips, into a sharper caricature than Cox would perhaps allow.

We need leaders who are laughing, though Suffering, Servants. We don't have them, and that is why it *appears* that youth has *no* heroes at all.[17] Of course they have them—escapist heroes, fantasy heroes. But, says Denny O'Neil, new editor of *Wonder Woman,* "Superheroes in general are not doing well."[18] Yet what he means is that television is stealing more and more of the kids' time. Woe betide the society that lets government take over television, as, from the industry's financial picture, it seems about to do. For, if the new experimental series of "documentary" dramas on CBS are any indication, we are in for a spate of animated whitewashings that will remove heroic images even further from the truth of man's aspirations than they now are. Anybody who has attended "A Talk with Mr. Lincoln" at the California Disneyland, or seen the televised preview of the whole panel of presidential robots, flawless with presence and charisma, from the Florida Disneyland, will appreciate what the possible excesses will be from government manipulators, who will certainly not be satisfied with whitewashing the Nuremberg trials in a Hitler "documentary," when they can utilize the superheroes of history, and make-believe, to mesmerize the populace into "clear-eyed" submission. Such a turn of events would be worse than the reverse, to which we alluded earlier, the revolutionary explosion of the "Buckingham guards," filled with the fury of Thing, Hulk, and Beast, ready to do battle for "truth, Justice, and the American way," and perhaps even God, Mother, and the Flag. It wouldn't be funny even to get hit with a bladder, a slapstick, or a wet noodle, if what this symbolized was a takeover by youth. After all, the Robins and Superboys outnumber the Clark Kents and Bruce Waynes. Inadvertently, Walter G. Hadley, a Big Little Book supplier, has, in that instance, pinned down the pedant who should have been pointing *up* the way instead of just pointing it *out.* The thing Mr. Hadley loved about big Little Books when he was a kid was that the "villain's evil gave glory to Good."[19] Well, who is evil today, Batroc, the manipulated villain who finally does go over to the side of Captain America, or the minions of Hydra, who got Batroc into his jam with Captain America in the first place? Perhaps some of us raised on our dignities won't want to choose the role of good caricature and will be forced by a painful ploy between government and private interest groups to accept one of the negative kinds of charisma, the villain, manipulated or manipulative.

Yet the charismatic art, the "magic art," of the cartoon world may yet save us. It "invokes deities." This is perhaps "one reason why the use of art for entertainment has been feared by authority in so many civilizations."[20] "To the chagrin of many an Army chaplain," Superman operated as "a symbol of a new patriotic faith" for the American G.I., during World War II.[21] Find the right—or wrong—icon, and you will have a saint or a devil, but charisma in any case.[22] "In the teaching of Christ," says the theologian Elton Trueblood, "genuine religion and genuine humor are conjoined."[23] The traditionist ought not to fear Rupert, a British cartoon animal who looks like Winnie the Pooh and who has been made a totem by some "hippies."[24] Even cartoon techniques are frequently a comfortable echo of, for example, the "heavy black stained-glass-window line," as used to draw the figures in *Little Nemo* and in *Li'l Abner*.[25]

The kinetic power ready to uncoil in the illuminated icon is there.[26] Perhaps cartoon icons may one day perform miracles again, as Picasso hoped paintings would do. As for the present writer, such a possibility is seriously found in a very fine psychedelic panel of Elric, in the May, 1972, issue of *Conan the Barbarian*.[27] Here we see Elric, the sorcerer, pounding back to his own universe on a magnificent blue stallion, with fluorescent pink exploding background. He is going home to fight evil, and, though our reflex utterance is, "Much good may it do him!" we can not help feeling at the same time that he must and will succeed. And this, in all wryness and yet conviction, is the way we responsively read our icon of Elric.

NOTES

[1]Fredric Wertham, *Seduction of the Innocent* (Rinehart, 1953), p. 176.

[2]Dixon Wecter, *The Hero in America* . . . (Charles Scribner's Sons, 1941), p. 421.

[3]*Ibid.,* pp. 9, 49 f., 135.

[4]Curtis D. MacDougall, *Understanding Public Opinion . . .*(Macmillan, 1952), p. 635.

[5]Stephen Becker, *Comic Art in America. . .*(Simon and Schuster, 1959), pp. 9, 14, 61.

[6]Jules Feiffer, *The Great Comic Book Heroes* (Dial Press, 1965), p. 13.

[7]Robert D. Field, *The Art of Walt Disney* (London and Glasgow: Collins, 1945), p. 11.

[8]George Herriman, *Krazy Kat,* ed. Joseph Greene and Rex Chessman, intro. E. E. Cummings (Grosset and Dunlap, 1969), p. 81.

[9]Lancelot Hogben, *From Cave Painting to Comic Strip* (London: Max Parrish, 1949), pp. 17, 19.

[10]Leroy A. Campbell, *Mithraic Iconography and Ideology* (E. J. Brill, 1968), p. 40. A discussion of certain Esquiline reliefs.

[11]*Wonder Woman* (May-June, 1972).

[12]Alton Ketcham, *Uncle Sam: The Man and the Legend* (Hill and Wang, 1959), p. 87; Hogben, *op. cit.,* p. 230.

[13]Wecter, *op. cit.,* p. 81.

[14]Lucy Lippard, *Pop Art* (Frederick Praeger, 1966), facing p. 170.

[15]*Op. cit.,* p. 8.

[16]Burne Hogarth, "Foreword," in Pierre Couperie, Maurice C. Horn, Proto, Destefanis, et al., *A History of the Comic Strip,* trans. Eileen B. Hennessy (Crown, 1968), p. 4.

[17]See Rabbi Abraham Shusterman, "Getting Along: Youth Suffers Dearth of Heroes," Baltimore *News-American*, Feb. 20, 1972. Big TV slave "kids" are the same way, says "Most Americans Have No Present-Day National Hero," *National Enquirer,* March 26, 1972, p. 5 (unnumbered).

[18]Letter to the author dated March 9, 1972.

[19]Letter to the author undated, postmarked June 27, 1969.

[20]George Perry and Alan Aldridge, *The Penguin Book of Comics*, rev. ed.

[21]*Ibid.,* p. 166.

[22]See Spencer C. Bennett, "Christ, Icons, and Mass Media," in Marshall Fishwick and Ray B. Browne, eds., *Icons of Popular Culture* (Bowling Green University Popular Press, 1970), pp. 91-92.

[23]Elton Trueblood, *The Humor of Christ* (Harper and Row, 1964), p. 125.

[24]George Perry, *op. cit.,* p. 214.

[25]Couperie, *op. cit.,* 205

[26]See *ibid., passim,* especially Burne Hogarth on how he conceived and executed the "total animation of the page" in *Tarzan,* trying to achieve "what Michelangelo achieved in the Sistine ceiling. . . . ," p. 213.

[27]*Conan the Barbarian,* Marvel Group No. 15 (May, 1972).

R. Charnigo

By BRUCE E. COAD
The Alger Hero

Hidden on one of the inside pages of a recent edition of *The New York Times* was a small article announcing the recipients of the Annual Horatio Alger Awards, an event that has been going on for some years now.[1] Certainly few people would dispute that the day has passed when simple country boys can become sole owners of large enterprises merely by climbing through the ranks from errand-boy to president. And contemporary sociologists, supported by much impressive statistical data, have been quick to point out that the majority of successful businessmen do not, and never did, struggle to the top solely by way of their own "pluck" and industry. Yet, even though it is no longer front-page news, a remnant of that era when the Carnegies, Rockefellers, and Vanderbilts were held up as national heroes who pulled themselves up by their bootstraps continued to cling to its place in the minds of many Americans.

The fact is that social engineering has largely replaced pioneering and profiteering as fertile ground for prospective national heroes—the Kennedys, Dr. King, and Malcolm X being examples that most easily come to mind; nonetheless, when the media refer to a "typical Alger hero," one can still consistently anticipate a formula-like report on the uniquely American phenomenon of successful businessmen whose careers, as the Horatio Alger Awards Committee puts it, "typify the results of individual initiative, hard work, honesty, and adherence to the traditional ideals, . . . who by their own efforts had pulled themselves up by their bootstraps in the American tradition."[2] Whether or not today's reader finds any degree of reality in such accounts, or whether he even has seen an Alger book, the rags-to-riches formula has clearly taken on mythic proportions in the past decades and has made "Alger hero" an American cliche.

With rare exceptions though, twentieth century literary critics have not considered Alger's fiction important enough to demand their serious attention. They not only have overlooked the possibility that he may be the most widely read author in American literature,[3] but with the exception of several recent studies largely concerned with disputing the accuracy of the three or four Alger biographies,[4] critics have singularly ignored the real message that Alger indefatigably portrayed for his young readers. Doubtless, Alger must be called extraliterary and "popular"—always for most "respectable" critics a pejorative term. Nor is it possible to argue that he is not a very minor influence in American literature; however, he still appears to hold a durable, if unexamined, position as a major influence in American folk ideals, thus suggesting that perhaps some critics and historians have unwisely neglected the substance of his fiction.

Despite this dearth of "respectable" scholarly interest, the Alger hero is decidedly still with us, if a bit tarnished and misunderstood. One has only to recall, for instance, the recent national interest in Texas billionaire, H. Ross Perot (would that the "H" have stood for "Horatio!"). Mr. Perot, who started seven years ago to develop a computer software company on an initial investment of $1000, has emerged today as one of the world's wealthiest men.[5] Curiously though, the national attention given to this latest "contemporary Luke Larkin" cannot in fact be attributed to his financial accomplishments, incredible as they might seem. Rather, in much of the newspaper and broadcast journalism that has discussed Mr. Perot's sudden-found prominence there was a consistent emphasis on his humanitarian exploits, e.g., his attempts to deliver mail and supplies to American prisoners in North Vietnam or his financial grants to experimental schools in Dallas, Texas.[6] Further, this same emphasis on the heroic nature in social responsibility was clearly apparent when in 1970 Mayor Carl Stokes of Cleveland, Senator Hiram Fong of Hawaii, and former governor Luther Hodges of North Carolina were selected to join such earlier recipients of the Horatio Alger Awards as Dwight D. Eisenhower, Ralph Bunche, Herbert Hoover, and Bob Hope.[7] It is implicit, then, that what is expected of the contemporary "typical Alger hero" is something more than a talent for piling up huge sums of money. He must reveal a new role: an acceptance of public responsibility far beyond making a profit. In the past one gained the status of "Alger hero" by working hard and maximizing profits. Now he cannot gain such a distinction without becoming deeply involved in furthering the aspirations of his fellow Americans.

Lest the confusion about the Luke Larkins and Herbert Carters be further compounded (indeed, more than a few of my students thought "Horatio Alger" was the name given to the young hero in the stories), it seems necessary to reassess (not debunk) the motives of those original characters, who in the process of becoming the most articulated element in the larger American dream of success, have lost a certain amount of their autheticity and are today being exalted for deeds they rarely performed.

A close reading of virtually any Alger novel would substantiate the claim that the humanitarian interests so prominent, for example, in Mr. Perot's activities were simply nonexistent in the original Alger version. On the contrary, in such novels as *Grit, The Young Boatman, Chester Rand*; or *A New Path to Fortune, Try and Trust,* and others, Alger reflects an almost obsessive predilection for money-making. And even though this observation has been made many times before, what seems to have been forgotten is that seldom does "our young hero" attempt to remedy social problems or improve the quality of life for anyone but himself (admittedly, these young men eventually manage to assume the overdue payments on their widowed mothers' mortgages). Consequently, after re-reading the novels, one might conclude that it is more accurate to label the Alger hero a "hustler" (an enterprising person determined to succeed in business at any cost) rather than a humanitarian—as the Alger hero is seemingly defined today.

There is little question that success in the Alger novel is virtually always measured in material assets and liabilities. Moses Rischin, writing

in *The American Gospel of Success*, puts it this way: Alger's economic
ethic "followed logically from the Puritan ethic which instructed men
to lay up wealth for the greater glory of God."[8] Of course, if one recalls the complementary side of the dual calling—what John Cotton
named a "deadnesse to the world,"[9] Alger's novels become revealing
examples of the tendency to make original seventeenth century religious doctrine into a secular expression. Consequently, when H. L.
Mencken argues that in original Puritan creed there was no distinction
between religious and economic interests, and that "later, Piety degene-
rated into hypocrisy and people seized this as the original,"[10] he is also
making a perceptive assessment of what goes on in an Alger novel.

Not only is money in the forefront of almost every story—how
much the hero earned on his first job, how much he spent on food
and rent, and how much of a fortune he indubitably gained (to the
penny), but the equation of the pursuit of happiness with the pursuit
of money is made explicit again and again. Simply noting the titles
of several novels may begin to suggest their content:

> *Five Hundred Dollars*
> *Herbert Carter's Legacy; or, The Inventor's Son*
> *Luck and Pluck; or, John Oakley's Inheritance*
> *Striving for Fortune; or, Walter Griffith's Trials*
>   *and Successes*
> *Timothy Crump's Ward; or, The New Year's Loan*
>   *and What Came of It*
> *The Tin Box; or, Finding a Fortune*
> *Tom Turner's Legacy; or, The Story of How He*
>   *Secured It*
> *Room at the Top; or, How to Reach Success,*
>   *Happiness, Fame, and Fortune*

The overriding single subject of these and numerous other
examples is money, and the things that go with money: power, re-
spectability, and position. In a typical moral argument that could
be dropped into almost any of these stories, Alger would say that
playing pool leads to drinking, which leads to idleness, which leads
to stealing, which sometimes leads to jail, but more often to poverty—
poverty being the ultimate punishment for Alger's villains and the
hell of his own brand of theology. It is not peculiar, for example,
that in *The Tin Box* the only punishment that young Philip Ross
incurs for stealing twenty dollars is the loss of his financially profit-

able position. Thus, while Alger's heaven may be little more than making a great deal of money, likewise everything and/or everyone in this world has a cash value, e.g., a boy who earns ten dollars a week is likely to consider himself twice as deserving as a boy who earns only five. Of course, it would be unfair to claim that Alger's heroes were without some ethical principles. But it nonetheless would also seem difficult for any perceptive reader today to imagine Herbert Carter or Bob Burton or any of the others as likely volunteers for service in organizations like VISTA or the Peace Corps. They simply did not have the time for such non-profit organizations.

Probably the most extreme example of Alger's obsession with the dollar is *Herbert Carter's Legacy*.[11] The story opens with a detailed description of young Herbert's "one source of income" and it sets the pattern throughout the novel. Alger's young man was employed to deliver letters and papers to families living some distance from the village post office (oddly, no young hero ever seemed to have time to "play" with the other boys, unless of course it was to compete for a prize—usually a Waterbury pocket-watch). As the reader might expect, Alger is careful to report any cash earnings to the exact penny:

> For this service he received a regular tariff of two cents for each letter, and one cent for each paper. He was not likely to grow rich on this income, but he felt that, though small, it was welcome. (p. 13)

Later, in a letter delivered to his own cottage, Herbert learns that his Uncle Herbert has died. The news excites considerable interest in our young hero:

> "Uncle Herbert was rich, wasn't he, mother?"
> "Yes, he must have left nearly a hundred thousand dollars."
> "What a pile of money!" said Herbert. "I wonder how it feels when a man is so rich. He ought to be happy." (p. 13)

That night Herbert fell asleep with thoughts of the inheritance well in mind:

> He dreamed that his uncle left him a lump of gold so big and heavy that he could not lift it. He was considering how in the world he was going to get it home, when all at once he awoke. (p. 18)

When Herbert actually attends the reading of his uncle's will, he soon learns that he is only one of many impatient relatives with hopes of changing their financial situations. This is how one of them described his intentions:

> "Well, I'm a second or third cousin. I don't know which. Never saw him to my knowledge. In fact, I wouldn't have come on to the funeral, if I hadn't heard that he was rich."
> (p. 31)

What young reader, selecting this novel from the Sunday-school library, would guess that Alger is *not* here preparing the ground for some larger attack on the callous greed of these people? And although Alger's fiction rarely displays any degree of subtlety, would not this be the precise time for "our young hero" suddenly to come to his senses and denounce this bizarre event? But curiously, the direction of the novel does not change. To be sure, Herbert is saddened that his legacy turns out to be nothing more than a trunk of old clothes and a "paltry one hundred dollars," but Alger makes it clear that neither Herbert nor the young reader should be disappointed:

> "I would rather make a fortune for myself than inherit one from another," said Herbert.
> "I respect your independence, my boy," said the lawyer, who felt favorably disposed toward our hero. "Still, a legacy is not to be despised." (p. 42)

If Alger's heroes seem obsessed with money-making, what might one expect from the villains? Interestingly enough, Alger carefully notes that, although both hero and villain are intent on financial success, it is "industriousness" that motivates the hero, while "greed" is what makes the villain run. Whether or not the perceptive reader can accept this thesis, the author makes it explicit that Herbert seeks his fortune with pluck and luck; Squire Leech seeks his fortune with covetousness:

> Squire Leech was a covetous man. He had a passion for making money, and he availed himself of all the opportunity which the country afforded, and until this moment he had fancied himself successful. But Temple's talk about the large amounts to be made in the city influenced his imagination. Why might not he, too, rise to a half a million in

five years? (p. 201)

As happens midway through almost every Alger story, Herbert decides to follow the well-worn path of other heroes and villains and heads for the city in search of his fortune and/or happiness. Before he departs he asks, "Is it easy to make money in the city?" "Yes, if a man is sharp and has some money to start with," answered the lawyer (p. 185).

Consequently, when Herbert finally arrives in the city, he is confident that "poor boys don't always stay poor" (p. 192), and he begins selling newspapers. Once again Alger takes pains to calculate the exact profits:

> The first day was not successful, chiefly because of his inexperience. He was "stuck" on nearly half of his papers, and the profits were less than nothing. But Herbert was quick to learn. The second day he cleared twenty cents. The third day he netted seventy-five. He felt now that he had passed the period of experiment, and that he would be able to pay his board. (p. 269)

Although there was probably little doubt in the young reader's mind that Alger would soon allow Herbert to find success, e.g., a financially profitable position in business, the remainder of the story is devoted to fleshing out the rags-to-riches formula. Alger makes it clear that his hero has "arrived" when Herbert returns to the village in time to rescue his widowed mother from Squire Leech who wishes to swindle her and gain the little cottage. Herbert displays his sudden adeptness in financial matters by shrewdly making this offer to the Squire:

> "If you choose to pay six hundred and fifty, we will sell. If you don't want to buy, we will make another offer. We will rent the house for ninety dollars a year. That is the interest on fifteen hundred dollars at six per cent." (p. 323)

Whether one likes it or not, then, *Herbert Carter's Legacy* does not appear to be part of what has been called "Alger's wonderful world of virtue rewarded."[12] Rather, in this novel and numerous others, the Alger hero is part of a society that has largely forgotten everything but money, making it the measure and source of all other value.

One may also argue that Alger is neither clear nor consistent about the ultimate significance of wealth. To be sure, at the outset of most of the novels Alger pays lip-service to the Puritan economic ethic: success comes to the thrifty, industrious young man because of his thrift and industry. And yet, despite this seemingly rigid formula of cause and effect, a close reading of the novels reveals that, in the end, the young hero routinely gains success because of an accident—saving a rich man's child from drowning, finding and returning a wallet to a wealthy businessman, or, as in *Grit, The Young Boatman*, finding a rich merchant's lost son.

Nor is there any convincing evidence that Alger holds providence responsible for such activities. Over and above the direct causal relation of virtue and prosperity, the Puritan tradition claimed the advantage of having God on its side. But conspicuously absent in most Alger novels is any indication that God might be even partially responsible for financial success. Instead, Alger asserted that "by pluck and luck" any young man could conquer poverty. One might look, for example, at the noticeably secular conclusion to *Struggling Upward*:

> So closes this eventful passage in the life of Luke Larkin. He has struggled upward from a boyhood of privation and self-denial into a youth and manhood of prosperity and honor. There has been some luck about it, I admit, but after all he is indebted for most of his good fortune to his own good qualities.[13]

The point is that Alger vacillates between his orthodox Puritan background and the reality of the social mores of the late nineteenth century. While he extolls work as virtuous in itself and the means to financial success, and accordingly, happiness, nonetheless the wealthy characters in the novels are more than often portrayed as avaricious or inhumane. Alger intrudes into *Herbert Carter's Legacy* to remind the reader,

> How a rich man like Squire Leech can deliberately plot to defraud a poor woman of a portion of her small income, you and I, my young reader, find it hard to understand. Unfortunately, there are too many cases in real life where just such things happen, so that there is really a good deal of truth to the old adage that prosperity hardens the heart. (p. 38)

But unlike Dickens in, for example, *Our Mutual Friend*, Alger was never quite convincing when he set out to attack society's lust for money. Indeed, he seemed obsessed with formulating a blueprint for financial success, and only infrequently did he allude to the humanitarian responsibilities (the "right" use of wealth) that traditionally went along with attaining success. Money spreads out to define the lives of virtually all the characters in his novels, heroes and villains alike. And even though in some instances Alger takes pains to introduce a "benefactor"—usually a successful businessman interested in giving aid to the struggling young men—that character invariably is part of a contrived ending or unbelievable circumstance that has little effect on the true shape of the book. Furthermore, no matter how often Alger reminds the reader that "prosperity hardens the heart," one cannot ignore the hollowness of such epitaphs when he recalls that in the last chapter of *Herbert Carter's Legacy*, and humerous others, Alger admits his hero into this supposedly sterile and "hardening" world as though he were opening the gates of paradise.[14]

In sum, the general line of my thesis is simple enough: money, and little else, is what makes the Alger hero run. A close reading of the novels provides virtually no evidence to support the claim that public service was ever an integral part in Alger's original formula for success. My contention, in this paper, is that critics who dwell, for example, on the "intense idealism of his parables, the selflessness of his heroes, and the kindly benevolence of their patrons"[15] have overlooked the larger and more prevalent thrusts of an Alger novel.

Further, by identifying today's "typical Alger hero" largely on the basis of his humanitarian activities, while glossing over the original heroes' singular talents for simply making money, scholars and journalists are adding confusion to an already dimly perceived piece of popular American literature. Perhaps this latest distortion of the Alger myth in part reflects the efforts of a society that is straining to create traditional heroes in a time when few are to be found.

NOTES

[1]*The New York Times*, May 7, 1970, p. 4.

[2]From "Opportunity Still Knocks," the publication distributed at the 24th Annual Horatio Alger Awards held May 6, 1970, at the Waldorf Astoria in New York City. Officially called The Horatio Alger Awards Committee of the American Schools and Colleges Association, this non-profit organization publicizes its concern about "the trend among young people towards the mind-poisoning belief

that equal opportunity was a thing of the past," and takes at its central purpose the need to provide tangible evidence that "the American way of achieving success still offers equal opportunity to all." After surveying campus leaders at some 500 colleges and universities for nominations, the Alger Committee, not surprisingly with Norman Vincent Peale presiding, selects approximately ten "successful" business and professional leaders to serve as examples that "the American Way is the highest type of human relationship conceived by the mind of man."

[3] Ralph D. Gardner, *Horatio Alger; or, The American Hero Era* (Mendota, Illinois, 1964), p. 346. Several other commentators have speculated on Alger's sales. F. L. Mott in *Golden Multitudes* (New York, 1947) conservatively sets the figure at sixteen or seventeen million. But Frank Gruber in *Horation Alger, Jr.: A Bibliography and Biography of the Best-Selling Author of All Time* (Los Angeles, 1961) argues that "estimates of their sales range from one hundred to three hundred million copies," and adds, "I am inclined to favor the latter figure" (p. 41). Certainly sales figures alone are not the whole story, since for each copy sold there were probably several readers, and frequently copies were passed on to succeeding generations.

[4] See, for instance, John Seelye, "Who Was Horatio? The Alger Myth and American Scholarship," *American Quarterly*, XVII (Winter, 1965), 749-756.

[5] For more complete accounts of Perot's financial prowess, see Arthur M. Louis, "The Fastest Richest Texan Ever," *Fortune*, LXXVII (November, 1968), 168-170, 228, 231; "Texas Breeds New Billionaire," (anon.) *Business Week* (August 30, 1969), 73-74; and Jon Nordhiemer, "Texan Fights Social Ills," *The New York Times*, November 28, 1969, p. 41.

[6] The opening remarks by Bill Lawrence on ABC's news interview program, "Issues and Answers," Sunday, January 11, 1970.

[7] See "Opportunity Still Knocks."

[8] Moses Rischin, *The American Gospel of Success* (Chicago, 1965), p. 21. See also Robert Falk, "Notes on the Higher Criticism of Horatio Alger," *Arizona Quarterly*, XIX (Summer, 1963), 151-167.

[9] Quoted by Perry Miller in *The New England Mind* (New York, 1939), p. 42.

[10] H. L. Mencken, "Puritanism as a Literary Force," *A Book of Prefaces* (New York, 1917), p. 235.

[11] Horatio Alger, Jr., *Herbert Carter's Legacy; or, The Inventor's Son* (New York, John C. Winston Company, no date available).

[12] Seelye, "Who Was Horatio?" p. 756.

[13] Horatio Alger, Jr., *Struggling Upward; or, Luke Larkin's Luck* (Akron, Ohio, Superior Printing Company, no date available), p. 280.

[14] See William Coyle's introduction to the Odyssey Press reprint of Alger's *Adrift in New York* (New York, 1966). The same conclusion has been voiced by Robert Falk, "Notes on the Higher Criticism."

[15] Seelye, p. 755.

By DAN PIPER
Dick Whittington and the Middle Class
Dream of Success

The story of the poor boy from the country who goes to the
city to make his fortune is one of the most popular folktales of
Anglo-American middle-class business society. Nowhere has it
flourished more widely than in the United States. We are familiar
with it in many versions, from the admonishments of Poor Richard
and the example of his famous progenitor, Benjamin Franklin, to
the novels of Horatio Alger, yesterday's *Saturday Evening Post*
romances, and today's cover-story in *Time* magazine.

Its tragic limitations have also provided the subject matter for
the stories and novels of many of our most respected authors, from
Hawthorne's "My Kinsman, Major Molyneux," Melville's *Pierre,*
Henry James's *The American*, Dreiser's *An American Tragedy*, to
Fitzgerald's *The Great Gatsby* and Faulkner's *Absalom! Absalom!*
Indeed, in its many forms it is perhaps the central myth of the Ameri-
can experience.

What are the origins of this familiar archetype? I decided to
begin my inquiry by studying the history of that popular English
bed-time-story hero, Dick Whittington. I found that over the years
he had become the best-known folk hero of the English middle-class,

and that his story embodied more than that of any other English
legend, the values of middle-class Anglo-American capitalistic society.
I also discovered that this story did not begin, as many English anti-
quarians have claimed, in medieval England. It can be traced back
through the mercantile capitals of medieval Italy, notably Genoa and
Venice, to the earlier centers of trade in the Middle East—and finally,
I believe, to Egypt. Its history, in other words, parallels the history
of the rise of modern international trade and geographic exploration
—of modern economic imperialism. The myth itself embodies the
values so dear to the capitalistic entrepreneur—the values of financial
risk, venture capital, rugged individualism and the aggressive search
for new and more profitable markets. Today when capitalistic society is more powerful and more on the defensive than ever before,
the antiquity as well as the historic vitality of this archetypal myth
needs to be better understood, both by those who would defend
that society as well as by those who seek to destroy it.

The best-known and most-fully developed version of this myth,
the English story of Dick Whittington and his cat, seems to have sprung
full-blown from the imagination of an Elizabethan hack-writer named
Richard Johnson. According to the Stationers' Register, an anonymous
play called "The History of Richard Whittington, of his lowe birthe
and great fortune" was played by the Prynces Servants and the license
to publish it was given to one Thomas Pavyer on February 8, 1605;
and a ballad or verse romance entitled "The vertuous lyfe and memorable death of Sir Richard Whittington, mercer, sometymes Lord
Mayor, of the Honorable City of London," was licensed to John
Wright, a printer, several months later. The fact that the story of
Whittington and his cat was already well-known by that date is shown
from a reference to "the famous fable of Whittington and his puss,"
that occurs in the play, "Eastward Hoe," by Ben Jonson, Chapman
and Marston that was first produced that same year. Both the ballad
and the play about Whittington have disappeared. But seven years
later a volume of verse-romances was published by the printer John
Wright, entitled *The Crown Garland of Goulden Roses*. It includes
the story of Whittington and his cat in ballad form, written by Richard
Johnson. Because Wright had already been Johnson's printer for some
years, it seems likely that Johnson was also the author of the earlier,
anonymous 1605 ballad. Back in 1592 Johnson had published an

extremely popular volume of stories celebrating the exploits of famous
London mayors, for the edification of young apprentices, and entitled
The Nine Worthies of London. It omitted any mention of Richard
Whittington, probably because at that time no remarkable events of
a romantic nature had yet been associated with him. During the interim,
that is between 1592 and 1605, either Johnson or some other city author
learned of the old story of the poor merchant and his cat—perhaps from
a visiting Venetian or Genoese merchant or seaman. Whatever the source,
this folktale became associated with the famous London Mayor and finan-
cier, Richard Whittington, who had died in 1423, almost two centuries
earlier. Within a few years the story of Whittington and his cat was to
become the most wide-spread popular expression of the dreams and
aspirations of the new rising English middle class.

Indeed, so pervasive has its popularity been over the past three
hundred years that one thinks immediately of the similar sudden and
dramatic popularity enjoyed several centuries earlier by Arthurian folklore. The Whittington theme expresses in popular form the values of
modern democratic business society much as the tales of King Arthur
and his knights, which sprang up and quickly swept over Europe around
the year 1100, embodied the quite different aristocratic and chivalric
values of medieval feudal society.

The significance of the Whittington story for English and American civilization can best be demonstrated by tracing its growing popularity through the many different forms of Anglo-American popular
entertainment. Johnson's *Crown Garland of Goulden Roses* went
through numerous editions during the seventeenth century. But
perhaps even more important was its retelling as a popular prose
romance, beginning around 1640. Before long it had become one
of the most popular titles in that flood of chapbooks, or cheap
reading for the masses, that began at the end of the seventeenth
century and continued well into the nineteenth century. As we
have seen, one of its earliest forms was also as a stage play. From
the London stage it moved quickly to that even more popular seventeenth century form of mass entertainment, the English puppet
theatre. We forget that even though the Puritans were successful
in closing the theatres during the Cromwell regime they never suc-
ceeded in shutting down the London puppet-theatres, where the
story of Whittington was one of the most popular works in the

repertoire. During the late eighteenth century the English puppet-theatre evolved into the famous Christmas pantomime, still today the most distinctive form of English middle-class popular entertainment. Students of the pantomime theatre report that Dick Whittington has been by all odds the most popular of all the English pantomime heroes.

A somewhat similar pattern can be traced in the history of Whittington's American reputation. Despite the fulminations of seventeenth-century Puritan divines against the reading of time-wasting romances, New England merchants and their ambitious young apprentices seem to have been as enchanted by the exploits of Dick Whittington as their English. Thus, in the records of a Boston bookseller for the year 1690 I have found more copies on order of Richard Johnson's *Crown Garland of Goulden Roses* than the tracts and sermons of more famous Protestant worthies. One of the first puppet-plays to have been performed in this country, in a Wall Street theatre in New York in 1749, was the tale of Dick Whittington.

By British law, most of the books read in the American colonies were imported from England. The enthusiasm of Americans for Whittington after the War of Independence can be seen from the frequency with which the title begins to appear as native printers now began to supply the demand for popular reading matter. Whittington was especially popular with workers in the new industrial mill towns that were springing up everywhere along the Fall Line. Thus, editions of Whittington from printers in the larger cities of Boston, New York and Philadelphia, soon began to be supplemented by editions published in Hartford, New Haven and Middlebury in Connecticut, Albany in New York, Dover in Delaware, Baltimore and Charleston.

A similar pattern can be observed in Great Britain where the continual stream of Whittington chapbooks published in London was increasingly supplemented by editions from the new manufacturing towns springing up to the north and west, as well as in Scotland. Like London, they too now required a steady supply of cheap labor—poor country boys in search of fame and fortune. Whittington's story, with its emphasis on democracy and the Puritan virtues of diligence, thrift and patient attendance to one's duty, expressed so perfectly the values of the new bourgeois mercantilism that no rival folk hero ever threatened Dick's popularity.

But how did the story begin? Here scholarship until now has been in disagreement. British historians who first investigated the Whittington legend hoped to show that it was indeed an authentic bit of English history. Thanks to their efforts we know a great deal about the real Richard Whittington who died in 1423, but I am convinced that this famous 14th century Lordy Mayor had only the remotest connection with the country boy of the legend. It has been claimed, for example, that the historic Whittington must have owed his great fortune to his cat, since Newgate Prison, which he generously rebuilt, once had a statue of Whittington with his cat at his feet, over the gateway. Investigation shows, however, that this was really an allegorical figure of Liberty, modelled after the Roman goddess of Liberty who was usually portrayed with a cat at her feet in the old Roman temples.

A second school of scholars, folklorists who collected European folktales extensively during the nineteenth century, have shown that the story of the poor merchant and his lucky cat is to be found everywhere throughout nineteenth century Europe although nowhere in such elaborate form as the English version. But no recent folklorist has studied the historic provenance of these European versions. By examining them in chronological order, I have concluded that the story originated in the Middle East and that its movement westward paralleled the westward migration of modern mercantilistic capitalism. All of the versions that can be dated prior to Richard Johnson's version, that is prior to 1600, are to be found only in Italy or the Near East. Thus the story of the merchant and his lucky cat is found in the writings of a Genoese story teller. It is found in the work of a German 13th century chronicler who associates it with the founding of Venice in the 5th century. It is also found in a thirteenth century history of Persia where the author associates it with the founding of a commercial port in the Persian Gulf. Thus it seems likely that the story came to Italy out of the Eastern Mediterranean, probably from Egypt to Rome by way of Carthage or Alexandria. Unlike most European folktales involving friendly animals, this story does not appear in Indian folklore, perhaps because early Indian society looked down so on trade and commerce; or perhaps because most early Indian trade with the west was by land rather than by sea. (The Whittington theme is always associated with an overseas venture.)

Reduced to its simplest terms, this ancient tale of the poor merchant who discovers that the common housecat can become a valuable export commodity, if he can find a land overrun with rats and mice where cats are unknown, illustrates one of the fundamental principles of business success. "Buy cheap and sell dear." Economic historians trace the beginnings of international commerce to ancient Egypt, on the grounds that it was the first society to abandon tribal, nomadic existence and create a stable, elaborately organized and specialized kind of civilization. It was able to do so because the regular, predictable flooding of the Nile, leaving a fertile valley for agriculture, made it possible for Egyptian rulers to tax and syphon off the surplus grain, which they then sold overseas to support an otherwise nonproductive ruling class of governors, military generals, and a priesthood. Egypt's royal wealth came from the sale of grain to the less fertile lands across the Mediterranean where food was in short supply. The grain had to be stored after harvest until it was needed, and protected from mice and other vermin. Hence the reason for Egyptian domestication of the small Libyan wild cat. In time both the harvest and the cat became major deities in the Egyptian pantheon, evidence of this importance. The cat was unique in that it was worshipped throughout Egypt as a beneficient animal, while elsewhere it was—and still is—regarded as a rare and strange beast usually associated with evil.

It seems quite likely then that the Whittington tale, in its earliest form, evolved naturally as a folktale in some ancient Egyptian port, perhaps first told by some early Phoenician or Greek merchant-seaman who served the Egyptian grain trade. Little of that folklore has been perserved. But it is said that the tale still survives in some of the old towns of present-day Iran.

If my conclusions are correct, then it is not surprising that the entrepreneurial impulse, with its emphasis on rugged individualism and a continually expanding market, has been so distinctively western a phenomenon. Nor is it remarkable that no versions of the Whittington story have been found outside the west, in Asia or the Pacific Islands or in American Indian folklore. In today's Britain the glamor of Dick Whittington is probably growing thin. Yet the children of the English middle class continue to meet him at their annual Christmas pantomimes and in their volumes of fairy tales, where Dick and his cat are invariably included as indigenous folklore heroes. In America after 1830 or so Whittington's popularity dropped off, as he was replaced by native examples of the "poor boy from the country" legend. First came Franklin's spectacularly successful autobiography, followed by the novels of Horatio Alger, by presidential campaign biographies, and popular accounts of the rise of the great American tycoons and merchant princes. Indeed the success of President Nixon today is a conspicuous reminder of the continuing vitality of this most pervasive of Anglo-American success stories.

R. Charnigo

By MICHAEL MEHLMANN
Hero of the 30's — The Tenant Farmer

During the 1930's American social values regarding capitalism, management and labor changed. Rather than idolizing Henry Ford's efficiency, any Mr. Jones who was hurt in any way by the hard times, probably identified with poverty. The real issue is that Americans who once valued materialism and production looked toward new ideals of endurance.[1] In the face of the depression and poverty few groups showed more endurance than tenant farmers. This made them heroic symbols of the popular culture of their times.

Despite the depression, attitudes toward farming were not greatly changed. Farmers remained self-sufficient with respect to what they needed for production. Horses and mules remained the chief sources of power.[2] Rexford Tugwell, Administrator of the Resettlement Administration, wrote "The people who stayed in the hills in their decent small houses, found year after year that competition from newly settled lands was harder. . . ."[3] By 1935 vast areas of rural America were in a state of shabbiness and disrepair. Farms were cluttered and run down, reflecting a deep-set state of poverty. Barns, outhouses, fences and grounds sagged under the weight of time. Even this atmosphere did provide some strength necessary for the future, as one tenant farmer said, "A human being has a right to stand like a tree has a right to stand."[4]

The popular culture of the 1930's tried to explain to the public what was happening. If our Mr. Jones read the newspaper, popular novels, or watched newsreels he learned about the Dust Bowl, the destruction of the "garden," and the problems of tenant farmers. For example, in John Steinbeck's *Grapes of Wrath*, Tom Casy, an Oklahoma poor white comments on the farm of a former friend, "If I was still a preacher I'd say the arm of the Lord had struck. But now I don't know what happened."[5] The same writer revealed to urban theater goers the itinerant farmer's desire to own his own farm in *Of Mice and Men*, as George tells Lenny about the farm they plan to own:[6]

> George's voice became deeper. He repeated his words rhyth-
> mically as though he had said them many times before. "Guys
> like us, that work on ranches, are the loneliest guys in the world.
> They got no family. They don't belong no place. They come
> to a ranch and work up a stake, and they go into town and
> blow their stake, and the first thing you know they're tail on
> some other ranch. . . . With us it ain't like that . . . Someday
> we're gonna get the jack together and we're gonna have a little
> house and a couple of acres an' a cow and some pigs and—"
> "An live off the fatta the lan'," Lennie shouted.

Tenant farmers organized the Southern Tenant Farmers' Union and carried out nationally prominent strikes in 1935 and 1936. The repression and terror that followed the strikes allowed urban factory workers to identify with tenant farmers whom they once considered remote. The leader of that union has told me that the public considered the issues according to the labor relations attitudes of the times and failed to see the latent populism involved.[7]

Populism or not, tenant farmers became prominent figures in the 1930's. Newspapers such as the rural *Earle, Arkansas Enterprise* and the *DeQueen Bee* of DeQueen, Arkansas, devoted copy to tenant farmers, as did urban newspapers such as the *Arkansas Gazette* of Little Rock, Arkansas, and *The New York Times*. Similarly, black newspapers, such as the *Savannah Tribune* also considered sharecroppers. Journals of opinion and magazines, such as *Fortune, New Republic, Newsweek, Saturday Evening Post, Crisis, Survey, Commonweal, Christian Century, Scientific Monthly*, and *Harper's* reviewed the lives and problems of these tenants.

Photography also served as part of Mr. Jones' learning experience. Books such as Erskine Caldwell's and Margaret Bourke-White's *You Have Seen Their Faces*; Dorothea Lange's and Paul S. Taylor's *An American Exodus*; Herman C. Nixon's *Forty Acres and Steel Mules*; and James Agee's and Walker Evans' *Let Us Now Praise Famous Men* reflected the human erosion of tenant farm life. The documentary photographer brought to the public the faces of the people and their homes; the nature of the land, as well as its contours. They explored the need for conservation of human and natural resources. To his photographer, Walker Evans, James Agee wrote:[8]

> Against time and the damages of the brain
> Sharpen and calibrate. Not yet in full,
> Yet in some arbitrated part
> Order the facade of the listless summer.

Documentaries and narratives also explained the social crisis. Book, such as Agee's *Let Us Now Praise Famous Men*; Norman Thomas' *Plight of the Sharecropper*, Charles S. Johnson, et. al., *The Collapse of Cotton Tenancy*; Arthur Raper's and Ira Reid's *Share-croppers All!* and *Tenants of the Almighty* and the Southern Tenant Farmer Union's pamphlet, *The Disinherited Speak*, educated Mr. Jones. Agee discussed his book in one of his letters, "My trouble is, such a subject cannot be seriously looked at without intensifying itself toward a centre which is beyond what I, or anyone else, is capable of writing of: the whole problem and nature of existence."[9]

But public opinion was not of one mind on this matter. Although sharecroppers represented symbols of strength, innocence and endurance to some, to others they represented personal failure and poverty. One cotton broker declared, "You can't entirely blame the planter. *Slave labor is necessary to cotton.* A decent wage would ruin the growers."[10] A writer for the *New Republic* reported a female comment, "Look at them. They live worse than pigs, and living with them we're turning into pigs."[11] Floyd Keeler reminisced, "The sharecropper's lot was not worse than that of the poor anywhere."[12]

All of the media brought forth various myths about tenant farmers. However, the concept of the tenant farmer as an "apprentice," who upon earning his own fortune would become his own master, was not true. The proportion of tenants over thirty-five years of age was constantly increasing during the depression—a trend which indicated that larger and larger numbers of those who had begun as tenants were unable to life themselves from poverty.[13] The fact that more blacks owned their own farms than whites, and more whites were tenant farmers than blacks, disproved another myth.[14] The belief in the laziness of tenant farmers was disproven through the vigor of their strikes in 1935 and 1936.

Throughout American history one form or another of tenant farming has always existed. In the extreme case it was slavery, and among poor whites there was indentured servitude. The Anti-Rent Wars in New York State serve as another example. High rates of tenant farming also existed during the era of America's westward expansion.[15] In 1936, the report of the National Resources Planning Board stated that, while approximately 30% of American farmers were tenants in 1880, by 1930 there was an increase to 63 percent.[16]

Who was this American, this tenant farmer? Like others, he was the object of many complex forces. During the first two decades of the twentieth century, tenant's farm plots decreased from 25 to 18 acres.[17] Tenants lacked adequate work stock. One tenant asked Governor Futrell of Arkansas for help in a letter stating, "I'll be frank I really failed on last years [sic] crop simply because my horse died during the crop season."[18] Tenants had over three-quarters of their acreage in cotton.[19] As the price of cotton fell, tenants could not meet their debts. In fact, 43 percent of the tenants were in debt before they planted 1934's crop.[20]

The depression reduced life to pitiful levels in the South. The price of cotton fell to a century low.[21] Dry weather prevailed and dust storms destroyed crops and feed. There was a fifty percent loss of per capita rural income while no similar decline occurred regarding fixed charges.[22] The per capita income in Arkansas, for example, was $175.26.[23] As taxes were high, farmers found it difficult to meet mortgage payments so that foreclosures were frequent. It is estimated that in 1933, 76 percent of all sales were "forced sales."[24] One citizen wrote Governor Futrell, "I have made every effort possible to save my 80-acre farm which will be certified to the state . . . unless I can raise $28.34 for taxes.[25] Farmers who lost their farms were forced to either become tenant farmers or hire out as day laborers.

As the news media, government and intellectual sources revealed the desperate living conditions of tenant families, the public became aware of their tribulations. Tenant families often lived in wretched hovels, unpainted and dilapidated. Many had leaky roofs and walls through which daylight could be seen and cold felt. Few households had any furniture. Sanitation was generally primitive. From DeQueen, Arkansas one tenant farmer wrote, "Now Gov Futrell If [sic] you dont come to our rascue we will starve inside of thirty days sure. . . ."[26]

The popular culture of the era presented the tenant farmer as an innocent struck down by economic forces beyond his control, but a part of the story was left untold. Social problems also worked to destroy tenant family life. For example, the declining numbers of marriages in Arkansas reflected the highest ratio of broken homes in rural areas for any southern states.[27] Yet tenants maintained large families and rationalized that large families were beneficial as large numbers of workers were needed for the crop season.[28]

Lack of education was also a serious problem. Approximately twenty percent of the rural males never attended school in Arkansas during the depression, while only 26 percent of rural Arkansas' children completed the eighth grade.[29] Tenants lacked faith in the virtues of education as it was irrelevant to their lives. One tenant said, "Five months of school is all I'm in favor of, because I need my children at home to help work the farm."[30]

Public health officials believed that public health was even more neglected than schools. Many poor rural people did not understand the need for, or could not afford, physical examinations. Thus typhoid fever and dysentery were common, tuberculosis claimed many victims and hookworm was prevalent. Tenants also suffered from malaria, venereal disease, pellagra and infected teeth and tonsils. The problem was compounded by the fact that there were fewer than ten doctors per 10,000 citizens in 1930 in Arkansas, as compared to a national average of 1 to 750 people.[31]

Poor living conditions and the lack of work forced tenants to expand their debts with their landlords. Upon the sale of the crop, debts had to be paid and tenants often received little as their debts mounted. Poor working conditions forced some tenants to leave

their farms and search for work.[32]   They usually moved within their
local counties. But few found life on the road satisfying. Moving
was costly in terms of time and money. Although the migrant farmer
was considered a folk-hero, the realities of migration further destroyed
social and familial relations as tenants were reduced to day laborers.[33]

In many ways geographical isolation was among the tenant's
greatest difficulties. Roads in rural areas were poor and transporta-
tion was often difficult. Mr. C. B. Baldwin told this writer that geographical isolation prevented New Deal agencies from reaching many
hardcore poor farmers. When tenants could travel, their social lives
usually centered about the Baptist, Methodist or fundamentalist
churches.[34] Unfortunately, one-third of the ministers of the tenants'
churches lacked theological training and usually earned a living through
farming or some other occupation.[35]

Despite the social acceptance of the tenant farmer as a hero of
the day, the churches reflected more traditional attitudes. For example,
the Southern Baptist Convention attributed the depression to the "Providence of God." Poverty was punishment for a prodigal people and economic recovery was dependent upon a religious revival.[36] Tenant farming was not the subject of any thorough investigation at any major Baptist
convention.[37] The Methodist Episcopal Board of Missions listed tenant
farming as a specific evil in 1936. Unfortunately, on the local level,
clergymen often sided with the planters against the tenants.

Lack of political power was another factor that bound tenants
to their situation. In Arkansas, a one dollar poll tax prevented them
from voting.[39] Intimidation by planter elements maintained this
social structure. Planters could do as they pleased as tenants needed
help in order to work. When conditions drove tenants to organize a
labor union for themselves, E. A. O'Neill, President of the planter
dominated Farm Bureau Federation, commented that people who
bothered about tenant farmers and their rights were well-meaning but
"soft-headed do-gooders" who simply did not understand the unlimited
opportunities open to all "free, white and twenty-one in the cotton
south."[40] *The Southern Agriculturist* commented:

> This publication, like the vast majority of farmers is in full
> sympathy with the man who works for wages . . . But because
> of the complexities of farming, there is no way to fit agricul-
> ture into its scheme regardless of what turn organized labor

might take.

When Americans considered the problems of tenant farmers during the New Deal they often assumed that the agencies which were set up to help the middle-class-made-poor would also serve tenant farmers. That did not occur as tenants lacked collateral for government loan programs or were not really considered in the Agricultural Adjustment Act. *The Sharecropper's Voice*, newspaper of the Southern Tenant Farmers' Union, commented:[42]

> Dressed up farmers, not a pair of overhauls [sic] in the whole crowd, immaculate white collars, spats and canes, knife-creased pants, pockets full of money riding in expensive automobiles and special pullman trains went to Washington to sing praises of the A.A.A. . . . The A.A.A. means nothing to poor folks.

Although the Agricultural Adjustment Act was considered an expression of grass roots democracy that educated tenants and allowed them voting powers, it was less than that. One county agent in the Arkansas Delta declared that he made all arrangements for the government with the landlords, and the landlords simply agreed to treat the tenants "right." The agent turned the tenants' A.A.A. checks over to the landlords, who forced tenants to endorse them. Sometimes A.A.A. checks passed directly from the county agent to local merchants to cover tenants' debts. One tenant wrote, "The planters tell us to sign or move. . . ."[43] Similar problems were involved in relief and PWA spending and administration.[44]

During the New Deal, politicians in the south feared that federal relief might create a new social class that would vote them out of power. For example, Arkansas' relief agencies withheld relief allotments from tenants in 1935.[45] Officials of the Resettlement Administration and the WPA in Washington were powerless to force local administrators to carry out programs. Arkansas' Senator Robinson did not allow New Deal relief agencies to function in Arkansas as he was close to planter interests and did what he could so that they would not lose their supply of cheap labor.[46] Huey Long's successful campaign through Arkansas in 1932, which elected Mrs. Hattie Carraway to the Senate, was not lost on Robinson. Nor was he unaware of Long's hatred towards him and he was sure Huey would campaign in the state in 1936 and turn the poor vote against him.

The tenant farmer who was a national hero was a white man. During the depression era segregation was a way of life which was nationally acceptable. The New Deal failed to change racial prejudices.[47] For example, one former New Dealer told this writer that, "There was no trouble as long as the two groups did not mix."[48]

With the coming of World War II the tenant farmer was forgotten. Despite the efforts of the Resettlement Administration and the Farm Security Administration, little was done. For example it was originally hoped to relocate 40,200 and after two years the RA had relocated 1,200.[49] Nevertheless, the RA's Information Division did much to reveal the quality of life on a tenant farm. For example documentary films were produced that were important and reached many people: Pare Lorentz' epics, *The Plow That Broke the Plains, The River,* and *Fight for Life;* Joris Ivens' *Power and the Land; The Land* by Robert Flaherty and *The Home Place,* directed by Raymond Evans. Classics of vocabulary photography reached many readers and often it is forgotten that the F.S.A. sponsored James Agee's *Let Us Now Praise Famous Men;* Archibald MacLeish's *Land of the Free; Forty Acres and Steel Mules* by Herman C. Nixon, Sherwood Anderson's *Home Town; 12 Million Black Voices* by Richard Wright and Edwin Rosskam; *Tenants of the Almighty* by Arthur Raper, and Dorothea Lange's and Paul Shuster Taylor's *An American Exodus.*

While tenants were obviously part of the public culture with the coming of the War, the symbol of the G.I. was supreme. The end of the War saw some former tenants dead while others took advantage of their veteran's benefits to reestablish themselves. Other tenants moved to manufacturing centers during the war and worked in war industries. Thus a rural-urban migration developed.

In our present urban oriented society, social pressure groups exist that represent tenant farmers. Aside from the charismatic Cesar Chavez, the rural folk hero has been forgotten. Urban oriented Americans fail to realize the present depth of rural poverty. The 1962 Manpower Report of the President pointed out that 11 million rural Americans, (1 out of 5), live in poverty.[50] These poor outnumber those in the cities. One wonders whether the recent migrants to our large cities often considered the "urban poor" are not also part of that American experience we have been discussing as the heroic farmer.

NOTES

[1]This is a generality made for the sake of communicating a point of view. Obviously there are various incidents to disprove these generalizations. See David E. Stannard, "American Historians and the Idea of National Character: Some Problems and Prospects," *American Quarterly*, v. 23, No. 2, May, 1971, pp. 202-220.

[2]U. S. Department of Agriculture, *Yearbook for Agriculture, 1970: Contours of Change*, (Washington, D.C., 1970), p. 2.

[3]Rexford G. Tugwell, *The Brains Trust* (New York, 1968), p. 67.

[4]Edward Steichen, *The Bitter Years, 1935-1941* (New York, 1962), p. viii.

[5]John Steinbeck, *The Grapes of Wrath* (New York, 1939), p. 55.

[6]John Steinbeck, *Of Mice and Men* (New York, 1937), p. 14.

[7]Correspondence with Henry L. Mitchell.

[8]James Agee and Walker Evans, *Let Us Now Praise Famous Men* (Boston, 1939), n.p.

[9]*Letters of James Agee to Father Flye* (New York, 1962), p. 95.

[10]W. Caroll Munro, "King Cotton's Stepchildren," *Current History*, v. 44, June, 1936, p. 67. Italics mine.

[11]Nathan Asch, "Marked Tree, Arkansas," *New Republic*, 87, June 10, 1936, p. 120.

[12]Floyd Keeler, "Share-cropper," *Commonweal*, 24, July 17, 1936, p. 303.

[13]Oscar A. Beck, Jr., "The Agricultural Press and Southern Rural Development 1900-1940," (Diss. George Peabody College for Teachers), 1942, p. 6.

[14]Earl Blake, "Farm Tenancy in Arkansas," (unpublished seminar paper for Business Administration, U. of Arkansas, 1939), p. 16.

[15]Paul W. Gates, "Homestead Law in an Incongruous Land System," republished in Carl Degler, ed., *Pivotal Interpretations of American History*. Vol. II, (New York, 1966), p. 8.

[16]U. S. National Resources Board, Land Planning Commission, "Report on Land Planning, Supplementary Report," Washington, D.C., 1936.

[17]Donald H. Grubbs, "The Southern Tenant Farmers' Union and the New Deal," (diss., U. of Florida, 1963), p. 19.

[18]Letter of R. L. Thompson to Governor Futrell, March 26, 1935. Futrell Papers deposited at the Arkansas State Historical Commission, Little Rock, Arkansas. Hereafter cited as *FP*.

[19]John Gordon McNeeley, "Tenancy in Arkansas," (U. of Wisconsin, 1941), p. 148.

[20]Charles S. Johnson, *et. al.*, *The Collapse of Cotton Tenancy*, (Chapel Hill, N.C., 1936), p. 11.

[21]*Agricultural Statistics*, 1940, p. 108.

[22]Charles F. Schwartz, "Income in the South," (diss. U. of Virginia, 1939) p. 45 and *New York Times*, March 3, 1933, Sec. 8, p. 1.; also see Gilbert C. Fite, *George W. Peck and the Fight for Farm Parity* (Norman, Okla., 1954), p. 18.

[23]Schwartz, *Ibid*.

[24]Rainer Schickele, *Agricultural Policy, Farm Programs and National*

Welfare (New York, 1954), p. 393.

[25]Letter of Mrs. Dora Sheppard to Governor Futrell, *FP*, June 3, 1933.

[26]Letter of W. S. Payne to Governor Futrell, *FP*, March 9, 1935.

[27]*Arkansas Gazette*, April 13, 1932, Sec. 1, p. 15. Also see Selz C. Mayo, "Rural Poverty and Relief in the Southeast, 1933-1935," (diss., U. of North Carolina, 1942), p. 407.

[28]McNeeley, *op. cit.*, pp. 113-114.

[29]U.S. W.P.A. Research Monograph No. 5, "Landlord and Tenant on the Cotton Plantation," Thomas J. Woofter, (Washington, D.C., 1936), pp. 131-132.

[30]Erskine Caldwell and Margaret Bourke-White, *You Have Seen Their Faces* (New York, 1937), n.p.

[31]Howard Odum, *Southern Regions of the United States.* (Chapel Hill, N.C., 1936), p. 370. Rupert Vance and Nadia Danielevski, *All These People, The Nation's Human Resources in the South* (Chapel Hill, N.C., 1945), p. 518.

[32]Beck, *op. cit.*, p. 6. Although there was a decrease of 235,000 tenants in the South from 1930-1940, most of these became migratory laborers and did not change their ownership status. Also see H. A. Wallace, "Wallace Points to the Dangers of Tenancy," *New York Times Sunday Magazine*, March 3, 1935, p. 4.

[33]*Ibid.*

[34]T. C. McCormick, "Rural Social Organization in South Central Arkansas," *U. of Arkansas College of Agriculture Bulletin.* (Fayetteville, Ark., 1934) p. 11. *FP*.

[35]E. deS. Brunner and Irving Lorge, *Rural Trends in Depression.* (New York, 1937), p. 317.

[36]Robert M. Miller, *American Protestantism and the Social Issues* (Chapel Hill, N.C., 1958), pp. 64, 116.

[37]Hugh A. Brimm, "The Social Consciousness of the Southern Baptists in Relation to Some Related Problems, 1910-1935," (diss. Southern Baptist Theological Seminary, 1944), pp. 11, 120.

[38]"Methodists Urged to Aid Sharecropper," *Arkansas Gazette*, November 21, 1936, p. 3.

[39]Discussion with local political leaders.

[40]Russell Lord, *The Wallaces of Iowa.* (Boston, 1947), p. 411.

[41]Beck, *op. cit.*, p. 183.

[42]Southern Tenant Farmers' Union, *The Sharecroppers' Voice*, June, 1935, p. 6.

[43]Richard Hofstadter, "The Southeastern Cotton Tenants Under the A.A.A., 1933-1935," (unpub. Master's Thesis, Columbia University, 1938), p. 38 and S.T.F.U.; *The Disinherited Speak*, (New York, n.d.), p. 3. David Conrad, *Forgotten Farmers.* (Urbana, Illinois, 1965), p. 66.

[44]Letter of Governor Futrell to Harry Hopkins, *FP*, "FERA, MISC Folder," September 30, 1934. Harold S. Myers, "Relief in the Rural South," *Southern Economics Journal*, 3, 1936-7, pp. 282-3. Letter of Duke Frederick to William Dyess, *FP*, September 30, 1933. James T. Patterson, *The New Deal and the States* (Princeton, N.J., 1969), p. 53. Letter of H. G. McCall to Mrs. W. E. Bond,

FP, "Welfare Folder B," December 8, 1934, Conrad, *op. cit.*, p. 34. *Arkansas Gazette*, April 11, 1934, p. 1. Mayo, *op. cit.*, p. 189.

[45]"Starvation in Arkansas," *New Republic*, 86, April 1, 1936, p. 206.

[46]*Arkansas Gazette*, November 14, 1964, p. 2A. Correspondence with Professor T. Harry Williams.

[47]Alber Kifer, "The Negro Under the New Deal, 1934-1941," (diss. University of Wisconsin, 1961), p. ix. Correspondence with Professor Paul Conkin. U.S. W.P.A., *Workers on Relief in the United States*, vol. 1, Philip Hauser, (Washington, D.C., 1938), p. 5. Rupert B. Vance, "The Negro Agricultural Worker Under Federal Rehabilitation," (mimeographed, n.d.), p. 220. Alexander W. Conn, "A Study of Negro Tenant Farmers in Pulaski County, Arkansas," (unpublished Master's Thesis, Fisk University, 1941), pp. 45, 51.

[48]Writer lacks permission to cite speaker.

[49]Statistics compiled from information in Futrell Papers and Resettlement Administration File at the National Archives.

[50]"New Shape of the Rural Labor Market," *Manpower*, vol. 1, No. 8, September, 1969, p. 21.

By LEVERETT SMITH

Ty Cobb, Babe Ruth and the Changing
Image of the Athletic Hero

Between 1919 and 1922 professional baseball underwent some
radical changes in public image in order to preserve its economic structure. These changes were three in number. First, professional baseball's understanding of its relation to American society at large was
drastically altered. Secondly, sweeping changes in the structure of
baseball's political community were instituted. Finally, baseball
became a new game on the field: a new style of play became popular.
In general, in its public image during these years, professional baseball
became less a sport explicitly identified with American culture at large,
with its democratic, capitalistic, egalitarian values, and began, in the
values it projected, to be a sport largely associated with authoritarian
values.

The Black Sox scandal and the public response to it had a great
deal to do with these changes. The scandal enabled professional baseball to undergo a public ritual of purification. Having discovered
itself to be a sick organism, it proceeded to first regain its health and
then to think of itself as healthier than the society of which it was a
part. In the course of dealing with the scandal it articulated its role
in the community at large as that of moral exemplar. After the
scandal, professional baseball presented itself as an alternative to

American society at large, more moral because it had solved the problems posed by pressure groups that too often made a democratic capitalistic society the prey of its strongest elements. And it had disassociated itself, in so far as was possible, from the taint of commercialism.

The changes which occurred in baseball's political order were closely related to the scandal itself. Just after the scandal broke, one writer expressed a hope which suggests the kind of change which took place in the political order. He hoped that both players and club owners might become convinced that "they are, or should be, all working for the good of baseball—an old time family gathering where hearts would be opened and cards laid on the table."[1] Here two metaphors which describe the nature of the political community rather differently sit side by side. The first, the metaphor of the card game, suggests commercially based activity, equals maneuvering to outwit one another. The second, the image of the family, suggests quite a different basis for the community: instead of equals at war, there is a hierarchy present that demands order and security. Finding a loose confederation, dominated by a kind of supreme court, insufficient for their purposes, baseball's leaders opted for a dictator, Kenesaw Mountain Landis, to whom they gave extensive powers. By May of 1922, the judge had established himself as the father-leader of a hierarchical society based on discipline. The players in the society were expected to be loyal, hearty chaps, grateful to the game for allowing them to rise to the top of their profession. Commercial considerations were to be left behind. Landis presided over a society opposed to the commercial society within which it existed and dedicated to transcending the commercial interests it found in itself.

This paper will concern itself with changes in the behavior of the citizens of this community, and players themselves, focussing on their public image, both on and off the field. Between 1919 and 1922 a marked change in offensive styles occurred. We want to see how the press (and presumably the public) accommodated themselves to this change and what values were lost, and gained, in the process. Since the home run hitting of Babe Ruth is popularly thought to have inaugurated the new offensive style, we will look particularly at his image, contrasting it with that of the leader of the old offensive style, Ty Cobb.

The basic difference in the offensive styles of Cobb and Ruth was a simple one: Cobb was a brainy player, Ruth a brawny one. Cobb's skill was thought to be scientifically acquired, Ruth's a natural talent. *Baseball* Magazine stated the opposition of styles nicely in a 1921 article.

> Baseball, year by year, had grown more scientific, more a
> thing of accepted rules, of set routine. This slow evolution
> of the sport displayed itself in batting, in the form of the
> bunt, the place hit and various other manifestations of skill.
> . . . Ty Cobb, perhaps, had as much to do with this batting
> evolution as any one man. Ty taught the world the supreme
> value of place hitting. . . . Under his magnetic leadership,
> batters tried for safe hits rather than long hits. . . . And
> because Ty was supreme among batsmen, no one even dared
> to question the merit of the system he employed.
> We do not intend to question it even now. To our mind,
> Ty is the greatest batter who ever lived. He was the supreme
> exponent of scientific hitting and science has a surpassing
> value in baseball just as in everything else. But every so often
> some superman appears who follows no set rule, who flouts
> accepted theories, who throws science itself to the winds
> and hews out a rough path for himself by the sheer weight of his
> of his own unequalled talents. Such a man is Babe Ruth in
> the batting world and his influence on the whole system of
> batting employed in the Major Leagues is clear as crystal.[2]

As the above quotation suggests, baseball, before Ruth began his slugging, was basically thought of as a science and a contest. The following quotation from a 1908 edition of *Baseball* Magazine equates this with the American community at large.

> Baseball is not merely an interesting and scientific game.
> It is the game which calls into play the dominant traits of
> Americans in its demand for agility, quick thinking, and a
> tremendous exertion and excitement. It is peculiarly popu-
> lar and fascinating to us because it means a contest, a personal
> hand-to-hand encounter. Baseball has all the elements of the
> personal battle which makes every red-blooded American itch
> to see a glove contest.[3]

Ty Cobb's own statement of what the game was all about echoes this in its insistence on separating baseball from mere games and equating it with war.

> When I played ball, I didn't play for fun. To me it wasn't parchesi played under parchesi rules. Baseball is a red-blooded sport for red-blooded men. It's no pink tea, and mollycoddles had better stay out. It's a contest and everything that implies, a struggle for supremacy, a survival of the fittest. Every man in the game, from the minors on up, is not only fighting against the other side, but he's trying to hold his own job against those on his own bench who'd love to take it away.[4]

Baseball for Cobb was a mirror of the commercial world, a competitive jungle in which each has an equal chance to survive. This is the system which results in the best coming to the top.

But a good player's most important asset was his brains. Cobb described the game as played by brainy players as a "game of hit-and-run, the steal and double steal, the bunt in all its wonderful varieties, the squeeze, the ball hit to the opposite field and the ball punched through openings in the defense for a single." These were all techniques of an offense which was "an act of skill rather than simply power." According to Cobb, this offensive style contained "fine, scientific nuances."[5]

These fine scientific nuances were dying out, according to articles which appeared in *Baseball* Magazine in 1921 and 1922. In them the decline of the bunt, the stolen base, and the three base hit were bemoaned. In all cases "slugging" was mentioned as a major cause of the decline. The following quotations give us some sense of the opposition of the two batting styles. "Bunting," it was said, "is the last word in batting skill because it marks the furthest departure from slugging, which is natural batting. Bunting is scientific batting because it is science which takes us from the beaten path of the merely natural." Base running, it was found, was not as much used as in the past because of the influence of slugging. "There cannot be any sort of sense in breaking a leg to steal a base when the giant at the bat is liable to make a four-base hit and chase the runner home ahead of him." The proper setting for power in the old style is seen in this description of the three base hit as "about the nicest hit of all, a line drive of terrific force, well placed between the outfielders, combined with nice judgement and speed of foot in baserunning."[6]

Ty Cobb was widely praised as the master of all these skills. Part of a poem printed in *Baseball* Magazine in June of 1920 is indicative of the sort of heroic qualities he was held to possess.

> He is Cobb! Cobb! Cobb!
> When they want a run he's always on the job;
> Either hits or sacrifices,
> When the game is at its crisis
> There's one man you can count on—Tyrus Cobb[7]

Four things in this stanza are indicative of the style of play Cobb represents. First it is significant that "they want a run" and not a lot of runs. Cobb's style of play was always to work for one run at a time: this would constitute a big inning. Cobb's style of play was work too: he was always "on the job." Thirdly, the sacrifice is an important offensive weapon for the heroic ballplayer to use. Finally, Cobb is the clutch player, to be counted on when "the game is at its crisis."

Above all Cobb was known as a player who used his head. One of the things this meant was that, though he did possess considerable natural talent, he constantly worked to improve his skills. Grantland Rice describes him as he was early in his career.

> . . . Ty Cobb . . . the greatest offensive player of the game
> . . . saw that he was only a fair base-runner, so he went forth
> alone, to slide and practice by himself, hours at a time. He
> kept plugging at this art until he knew that he could handle
> himself around the bases.
> Shortly afterward he began to find that he was weak against
> lefthanders. . . . At morning practice he got all the left-hand-
> ers he could find to pitch to him. And if there were none avail-
> able from the team he would pick up corner lotters or camp
> followers, and set them to work, blazing away at his weakness.[8]

The man who compiled the highest batting average of all time was admired by his contemporaries not for his talent but for the hard work he put in acquiring the various skills of scientific play.

The essence of Cobb's style of play lies in his advice to others: "Scheme, scheme and keep scheming."[9] Here he is the ultimate capitalist, his only goal to get ahead by outthinking his opponents. His extraordinary inner directedness can be seen in the following statement, quoted in *The Sporting News* in 1919.

> Although the game has grown faster and more scientific in
> my mind, there has not been the individual improvement you
> might look for. The boys of today play scientific baseball
> because it has been taught them, not because they dope it
> out themselves. They don't study the game like young doc-
> tors or young lawyers or engineers study their professions.
> After a game these kids are through with baseball until the
> next day. They don't take their chosen profession seriously
> enough. My success was due entirely to self-dedication and
> study.[10]

There is no role for a community to play here; the statement seems
totally individualistic.

The emergence of Babe Ruth as a slugger in 1919 had a great
deal to do with changing the public image of the ballplayer as set by
Ty Cobb. He was an awesome player in a way that Cobb could not
hope to be. In 1920, for instance, playing in his first season for the
New York Yankees, he hit more home runs than any other team in
the American League.

His home run hitting was thought to inaugurate a new style of
play, but opinions on the importance and permanence of this style
varied. One school felt that Ruth's style of hitting made him a freak
and "an accident." This was the opinion of many of the exponents
of scientific baseball. "Mere" sluggers were generally depreciated, as
in this poem from a 1920 *Sporting News*.

> His feet were like a pair of scows,
>   But he could hit.
> There was a void behind his brows,
>   But he could hit.
> He fielded like a four-wheel hack—
> And yet he always got the jack,
>   For he could hit.[11]

This player is attacked because he can't play scientific ball. Some
people felt Babe Ruth fit this mold. They maintained that "baseball is an athletic science that requires nine men working in harmony
to produce teams of championship caliber" and that Ruth disturbed
that harmony. The following is a representative comment.

> Ruth is a third-rate outfielder. As a base runner he is in a
> class by himself. I'm not complimenting him, either.

> As a batter, Ruth is an accident. He never plays inside
> baseball at the plate. He goes up trying to take a swing on
> every strike, a style that would cause any other player to be
> benched. He either knocks home runs or strikes out. Any
> man who strikes out as many times as Ruth did last year can
> never be classed as a great hitter.[12]

Ruth was defended from this kind of criticism in two ways. First
it was suggested that he was actually a good ballplayer in terms of
the old standards; he was a fine base runner, smart ballplayer, and
good fielder. Then it was argued that, although his hitting style
was rather heretical, he had arrived at it through the same process
of hard work and study that was attributed to Ty Cobb.

Baseball Magazine wondered how to fit Ruth's slugging into
their scheme of the evolution of offensive techniques in baseball.
The title of one of their articles on the subject is suggestive: "The
Home Run Epidemic." This article saw the phenomenon as funda-
mentally a change in batting styles. Ruth "has taken the place hit
[Cobb's specialty] from its pedestal as the batter's univeral model
and has set up in its place the home run."

> . . . Can there be any doubt that Babe Ruth was the man who
> showed the world the value of the circuit clout? . . .
> A leader in any field speedily obtains a following. . . . We
> do not mean to contend that the chop hitter who chokes up
> on his bat and punches out an occasional feeble single is hitting
> any more home runs than he ever did. But we do say, and the
> records bear us out, that almost every batter who has it in him
> to wallop the ball, is swinging from the handle of the bat with
> every ounce of strength that nature placed in his wrists and
> shoulders.
> . . . Babe has not only smashed all records, he has smashed
> the long-accepted system of things in the batting world and
> on the ruins of that system he has erected another system or
> rather lack of system whose dominant quality is brute force. . . .
> Does Babe's advent into baseball herald a new era of de-
> velopment? We cannot say. For a time, at least, the old
> order of things is in complete eclipse. . . . We are in for a
> true carnival of home run hitting which evidently has not
> yet reached its peak.[13]

The use of such metaphors as "epidemic" and "carnival" to describe
what was taking place shows that *Baseball* Magazine saw Ruth's style

as a kind of catastrophic interlude in the orderly progressive development of baseball styles.

Others were more able to see Ruth's slugging as the basis of a new and lasting offensive style of play. *The Sporting News* suggested

> That many batsmen are following Ruth's system is an open fact, and it will be only a short time when big league teams will encourage one or more in the line-up who possess the ability, which means giant strength and a keen eye, to try for homers every time, . . . There is no reason why George Ruth should have a monopoly or divine right to absorb all the glory and home runs derived from this style of hitting. If club owners and managers come to the conclusion that this mode of attack is effective and really a valuable asset in winning games, then there will be a general training in that direction and in a few seasons the woods will be full of more or less Babe Ruth style of swatters.[14]

The question of whether or not slugging is winning baseball is crucial here and it was a real question in 1919 and 1920, when the teams on which Ruth played did not win pennants. Many writers delighted in juxtaposing their own sense of the awesomeness of a Ruth home run ironically with the fact that it did not affect the outcome of the game. Christy Mathewson discussed the relation of slugging to winning seriously in the New York *Times.*

> There seems to be a great demand these days for star sluggers. There is no doubt of their value to a team, and the man who can rap out a home run frequently furnishes the fans with the most spectacular play in the game.
>
> But from the point of view of winning contests, my experience has taught me to prefer an aggregation of good baserunners to a batting order of hard hitters. I believe the former can do more to help a pitcher win games. . . .
>
> When a man is pitching for a team of baserunners he knows that every time a player with a reputation for stealing bases gets on the base, with half a chance, he is pretty sure to score a run. Then, too, when a club has a name for possessing base runners it helps to get the opposing pitcher's goat. He has to devote a lot of his energy to watching the men on the circuit and has less to devote to his pitching.
>
> On the other hand, a hard hitter who is slow on the bases is only a hindrance.[15]

This puts the case against the slugger well. A little more than a year later, Hugh Fullerton spoke of a heated argument among ball players and managers "concerning the value of long distance hitting and its effect upon baseball teams and baseball leagues." Fullerton felt that whether or not one argues for or against slugging depends entirely on whether or not one is on the same team with a slugger. He pointed out that the fans love slugging but suggested that "there may be a sharp reaction of sentiment when the fans discover that long-distance hitting is not winning baseball, but even that is doubtful." He concludes that "the real baseball is the middle ground, the judicious mixture of real baseball and slugging, with the manager deciding when and how the batters shall hit."[16] This suggests that things are beginning to change. Fullerton has moved the "reality" of baseball more toward the style of the slugger, even though his language is inadequate for this task. Slugging is becoming a legitimate tactic, even in the minds of the defenders of the old style. With it the qualities of strength and speed, natural talents as opposed to acquired skills, are gaining in value.

Ruth's own personality, as presented in the press, underlined these qualities and gave them human perspective. They come to suggest the ideal citizen of a hierarchically structured authoritarian community rather than the ideal citizen of a democratic, egalitarian, capitalistic community, as Cobb was.

Ruth was first presented as fitting the same mold as Cobb. As we have seen, both were shown to have worked hard to perfect their dissimilar batting styles. Both presented themselves as Ben Franklin types; proof of the faith that American society works. The effort to picture Ruth as a shrewd capitalist was a failure though, and the press soon abandoned its efforts to present him as one. One periodical remarked that "in winter he manages his cigar factory in Boston and is possessed of shrewd business sense as well as a sense of humor."[17] But this article fails to give any examples of his "shrewd business sense" other than the existence of the cigar factory and goes on to describe his sense of humor. Much the same thing happens in the following article.

> His [Ruth's] outlook on life is kindly but shrewd. He has
> various sources of income in addition to his salary and he is
> not spending all he makes. When baseball finishes with him

> Ruth will have money. Being a likeable young man he will
> also have friends who are willing to do real services for him.
> He will probably have his choice of a dozen good business
> offers.
>
> And he may turn them all down and decide to go it alone
> in some field of big business. If he does his admirers will
> expect him to make good. They say he has business sense.[18]

Again, his business sense was not documented. It seems only a pious hope in the minds of his interviewers.

Images that involve the natural, the instinctual and the childlike seemed to stick to Ruth more easily. He was pictured as a natural force, as a man who plays the game for love, not money, as a kind of foolish or simple person, and finally as a child. His knowledge of baseball was, we learn, instinctive rather than learned. That a player of this sort should be the largest gate attraction in the game was something new. The greatest players before had always had great talent, of course, but always they had worked and worked to improve and perfect their talent. This Ruth did not bother to do.

One of the things that drove Ruth, according to writers, was his love for the game of baseball. Hugh Fullerton writes of this quality in Ruth in *American* Magazine.

> In the past two years the baseball public of New York has
> fallen into the same habit. The fans flocked by millions to
> see the Yankees play ball, apparently caring little whether the
> team won or lost, so long as Babe Ruth made a home run.
>
> Yet "Bambino" himself is exactly the opposite. With him
> the game is the thing. He loves baseball; loves just to play it.
> I remember one day in Boston, when he was with the Red Sox,
> fighting for a game which meant perhaps the winning or the
> losing of a championship. He started in the game as an out-
> fielder, stepped into the breach as a pitcher, and finally won
> the game with a smashing hit.
>
> It was almost dark when some of us emerged from the park
> and started downtown. Two blocks away, a bunch of kids
> was assembled in a vacant lot, playing ball. And there was
> Babe, hitting the ball, just for the fun of it; just because he
> loved it; not to win something, or to keep from losing some-
> thing, but just for the sake of doing it.[19]

Here we find that Ruth was interested in playing baseball, not merely working at it. This was what his "love" for the game seemed to mean.

It is hard to imagine Ty Cobb in a sandlot game, with his "scheme, scheme and keep scheming" motto for human action. Ruth himself explained his behavior with reference to a love of baseball. On the occasion of being suspended for five days for arguing with an umpire, Ruth made the following statement.

> I do not regret being out of the game because of the money it costs me. I really don't need the money, but I do love to play baseball. For that reason it hurts when I can't get into the game.
>
> Another thing that hurts is the criticisms. Some persons are saying that I welcome the suspensions because it gives me an alibi for not equalling my home run record of last year. That is ridiculous, as I realise that that is impossible. Others claim that I have a "swelled head." My friends know different. I want to be in there every minute because I love to play baseball.[20]

Here Ruth uses his love of the game to remove himself from the suspicion of having commercial motives for his actions.

These kinds of images center eventually on the image of Ruth as a child. Ruth was defended against his detractors by being described as a child at play.

> Ruth is nothing if not a big grown up kid. Nobody in camp is working harder than he. He runs out every hit as if sprinting for a base knock in the real show and already runs them out past second base. Afield in fly chasing Ruth has shown a judgment and speed that matched the best efforts of Sammy Vick. Samuel was one of the speediest of Huggins' 1919 aggregation.
>
> Babe is working to improve his speed and range as instance a sample of his day's work. After his hitting practice he indulged in about an hour's "shagging" of fungoes while the infielders practiced fielding. Then Ruth came in to third base for a half hour more. He finished up the day with a few clownish antics for the benefit of the grand stand managers.[21]

Without the first and last sentences, this could be a paragraph about Ty Cobb. But the two sentences give the activity an entirely different context. Here is one final word on Ruth as a child. This particular passage concerns the size of his head and the effect that being a celebrity has had on him.

> What kind of a fellow is Babe Ruth? That is a question I have
> been asked hundreds of times since Babe hogged the sporting
> spotlight. Ruth's remarkable ability to hit home runs has made
> him the most discussed individual in the history of the game.
> Thousands of fans wonder what kind of a fellow he really is,
> when not engaged in busting them over the fence.
>   No doubt a great many people have the impression that
> Ruth feels his greatness. Nothing could be further from the
> truth. Ruth is a big, likable kid. He has been well named,
> Babe. Ruth has never grown up and probably never will. Suc-
> cess on the ball field has in no way changed him. Everybody
> likes him. You just can't help it.[22]

Ruth the child is the perfect representative citizen of Judge Landis'
kingdom. With this picture of Ruth the change of the community of
professional baseball from a community identified with a democratic
capitalistic world to a community which sees itself as authoritarian
and above commercial concerns is complete. Far from being a capitalist engaged in competition, Ruth is a child exercising his talents
out of love for the game. Professional baseball had become a big,
happy family.

NOTES

[1] *The Sporting News*, September 30, 1920.

[2] F. C. Lane, "The Home Run Epidemic," *Baseball* Magazine, July 1921,
pp. 339-340. See also F. C. Lane, "Natural Slugging vs. Scientific Batting," in
the August 1922 edition of *Baseball* Magazine.

[3] Quoted in Douglas Wallop, *Baseball: An Informal History* (New York:
W. W. Norton & Co., 1969), pp. 50-51.

[4] Ty Cobb with Al Stump, *My Life in Baseball—The True Record* (Garden
City: Doubleday & Co., Inc., 1961), p. 280.

[5] *Ibid.*, p. 145.

[6] F. C. Lane, "The Bunt as Scientific Batting," *Baseball* Magazine, May 1921,
pp. 572-573. *The Sporting News*, April 6, 1922. F. C. Lane, "What's Wrong With
The Three Base Hit?" *Baseball* Magazine, June 1922, p. 304.

[7] This is the last stanza of a ten stanza poem printed in *Baseball* Magazine,
June, 1920. Other representative poems appear in *The Sporting News*, Nov. 6,
1919 and Nove. 27, 1919.

[8] Grantland Rice, "The Swelled Head: Stories of Men Who Have Suffered
From It," *American* Magazine, October, 1919, p. 203.

[9] *My Life in Baseball—The True Record*, p. 173.

[10] *The Sporting News*, October 23, 1919.

[11] *The Sporting News*, May 20, 1920.

[12]*The Sporting News*, January 19, 1922.

[13]"The Home Run Epidemic," pp. 340, 372. This article was condensed in *The Literary Digest* (69), June 25, 1921, 51-52, 54 under the title "The Babe Ruth Epidemic in Baseball."

[14]*The Sporting News*, August 25, 1920.

[15]New York *Times*, February 8, 1920.

[16]*The Sporting News*, May 26, 1921.

[17]"A New Hero of the Great American Game at Close Range," *Current Opinion* (69), October, 1920, 478.

[18]Sidney Reid, "Meet the American Idol!" *The Independent* (103), August 14, 1920, p. 194.

[19]Hugh Fullerton, "The Ten Commandments of Sport, and of Everything Else," *American* Magazine, August, 1921, p. 78.

[20]New York *Times*, June 22, 1922.

[21]*The Sporting News*, April 1, 1920.

[22]*The Sporting News*, February 2, 1922.

By GERARD O'CONNOR

"Where Have you Gone,
Joe DiMaggio?"

Simon and Garfunkel felt it. And so did Santiago. Struggling
with the huge fish, the old man of the sea inspires himself: "I must
have confidence and I must be worthy of the great DiMaggio who
does all things perfectly even with the pain of the bone spur in his
heel." Malcolm X felt it. On June 22, 1937, the night that Joe Louis
knocked out Jim Braddock, Malcolm X "like every Negro boy old
enough to walk wanted to be the next Brown Bomber."
They all felt a commitment to, a belief in, and identification
with a professional athlete that transcended, overwhelmed, rendered
insignificant all the phoniness, the greed, the dehumanization of American sports. That athlete was not only better than all the rest, he was
different from them and far above them. That athlete personified
the dreams of their youth, realized the hopes of their people. That
athlete expressed in ritualistic and symbolic terms an ideal that was
both personal and cultural, unique and archetypal.
To Eldridge Cleaver, Muhammed Ali is a "genuine revolutionary,
the black Fidel Castro of boxing." In crushing Floyd Patterson, the
"leader of the mythical legions of faithful darkies who inhabit the
white imagination," Ali inflicts a "psychological chastisement on
'white' white America similar in shock value to Fidel Castro's at the
Bay of Pigs." To John Updike as a boy growing up in Pennsylvania,

Ted Williams was a name that "radiated, from afar, the hard blue glow of high purpose." Seeing Williams blast one out of Shibe Park, Updike felt that a Williams home run was "qualitatively different from anything anyone else might hit." Nearly twenty years later when Ted Williams took the last swing of a career spanning four decades, and drove a Jack Fisher fastball 400 feet through an east wind into the seats, John Updike—poet and novelist—was in the stands, screaming, shouting, and weeping.

Max Lerner has dismissed this kind of response as arrested development, a symptom of the eternally juvenile mind which the cult of American sports perpetuates. Although he recognizes that the bullfighter expresses ritualistically and symbolically the tragic meaning of life for the Spanish, Lerner, ironically, fails to understand the ritualistic and symbolic expression of a sports hero to an American. To a revolutionary like Cleaver, Muhammed Ali expresses the dignity, the pride, and the power of blackness. To a writer like Updike, Ted Williams expresses the talent, the intensity, and the dedication of the artist. And to folk-philosophers like Simon and Garfunkel, Joe DiMaggio expresses the spirit, the courage, and the style of the mythical folk hero.

The athlete-hero is above all else the great individual. Yet each in his own way defines his age, personifies the spirit of his times. Certainly Babe Ruth, Red Grange, and Jack Dempsey are as indelibly and evocatively the 20's as the speakeasy, the *Spirit of St. Louis,* and Valentino. Similarly, Joe Namath, Arnold Palmer, and Bill Russell are as indisputably the 60's as long hair, Middle-America, and Watts. It is easy to refine Emerson: there is properly no sports history, only biography.

These three characteristics—athletic excellence, charismatic personality, and eponymous symbol—crystallize for the first time in American culture in the legendary Hobey Baker. A product of the Main Line in Philadelphia and St. Paul's, Hobey Baker played football and hockey for Princeton from 1910-1914 with a style, skill, and *panache* that were never seen before and have never been seen since. F. Scott Fitzgerald anointed him in *This Side of Paradise* and George Frazier, nearly fifty years after his fatal plane crash, canonized him: "The image of him remains as it was in the swiftness and sinew of his youth, when, of all college boys, he was the most golden and godlike." As Arthur Mizener pointed out in the official hagiography, Hobey

Baker, "with his almost incredible skill and grace, his perfect manners, his dedicated seriousness, was the nearly faultless realization of the ideal of his age."

The image of the athlete as hero has changed somewhat from the *noblesse oblige* of Hobey Baker to the I'm-the-Greatest of Muhammed Ali; from the rich, blond, aristocratic gentleman to the poor, black, proud militant. These two paradigms of antithetical ideals suggest that this change has been revolutionary, and indeed it has. But this revolution is more like the Industrial than the Russian: that is, it evolves more than it erupts; it moves by stages, not explosions. Thus to understand the significance of Ali today, as Eldridge Cleaver makes clear, one has to go back to Joe Louis; similarly, to appreciate Joe Namath today, one has to go back to Babe Ruth, Red Grange, and Jack Dempsey.

The Sultan of Swat, The Galloping Ghost, the Manassa Mauler. These flamboyantly alliterative sobriquets may denote Ruth, Grange, and Dempsey, but they also connote an age. An age of excess, of excitement, of extremes. A murder-a-day depleted Chicago, and Murderers Row filled Yankee Stadium. Bryan inherited the wind of defeat from Darrow, and the Lone Eagle soared, as The New York *Evening World* proclaimed, to the "greatest feat of a solitary man in the records of the human race." *The President's Daughter*, the story of Warren Harding and Nan Britton, was a sensational best seller, while Valentino's Funeral was an epic spectacle. Fatty Arbuckle was destroyed, but Sacco and Vanzetti were immortalized. If there were no Babe Ruth, Red Grange, and Jack Dempsey in this age, then it would have been necessary to invent them—and in a sense that's what really happened. Ruth once suffered a hot-dog bellyache that was heard around the world, Grange was proposed for Congress after his junior year at Illinois, and Dempsey, who hopped freights to get to his first forty fights, made $8,450,000 in his next five. The Ruth who "called the shot," the Grange who raced through Michigan for four touchdowns, the Dempsey who refused to go to a neutral corner; this is the stuff of which the writers made heroes, and the people made myths. Number 77, The Long Count, and the Ruthean clout are the gilded monuments of our mythology that fifty years of sluttish time have not besmear'd.

Grange, Ruth, and Dempsey were popular heroes, national idols, legends in their own colorful times. And certainly the Twenties were colorful times—but the color was white. By refusing to fight his most formidable challenger, black Harry Wills, Jack Dempsey preserved the "color line" backlashed into existence by the Great White Hope response to Jack Johnson. Similarly, Babe Ruth's real challenger, Josh Gibson, hit his uncounted homers for the Homestead Grays in the Negro National League. It is doubly ironic then that the next genuine athlete-hero in America is a black man and that his rise to Fame is greatly effected by the government that not only champions Team Spirit, but also segregates its own servicemen.[1] The paradox resolves: faced with the extreme likelihood of Hitler's Max Schmeling knocking out the heavyweight champion Jim Braddock in their proposed match, the Powers-that-Be match Braddock with Louis. In 1937, Black is at least more beautiful than Aryan White.

The career of Joe Louis is a microcosm of the black experience in America. When he knocked Braddock out, "cataclysmic celebrations took place in Black communities everywhere."[2] And when he destroyed Schmeling in 1938, the whole nation erupted. For the rematch between Schmeling and Louis was more than a political showpiece between Nazi Germany and the United States, it was the symbolic confrontation of the Master Race and the American Dream. Louis won not only a great victory for himself and for all black people, but for country, church and flag. And, apparently, Louis accepted this role unquestioningly. For over the protests of the black power leaders of the day, Louis became an official spokesman for the Cause: "He made himself a living legend when at a Madison Square Garden rally in 1942, in uniform, he pronounced the words which became a rallying cry of World War II. 'We'll win because we're on God's side.' "[3] Unconsciously Louis was creating that image of himself which white middle America would accept and preserve. As the Archie Bunker *persona* remarks in the Lenny Bruce monologue, Joe Louis was indeed a "credit to his race."

The year that Louis knocked out Schmeling, 1938, was also occasioned by the election of Clark Gable as "King" and by an arrival from the exploding planet Krypton. The age of the super-hero had dawned, and the age of collectivist enterprise, such as that of the Gas House Gang, had dimmed. As Jules Feiffer has pointed out in his discussion of Superman, after several years of the Depression "it was apparent you had to be super to get on, Horatio Alger could no longer make it on his own." Paralleling the rise of the super-hero of the comics is the appearance of the modern super-star of major league baseball. In the late 30's two players, as counterpointed in personality as they were close in ability, emerged to dominate the most popular of American games—they were Joe DiMaggio and Ted Williams.

The mystique of the "great DiMaggio" is perhaps the most romantic in American sports. The son of a poor Italian fisherman, DiMaggio became Jefferson's natural aristocrat on the field of play. His grace as a ballplayer is still the standard, the touchstone, against which that of every young star is compared and condemned. DiMaggio earned his poetically appropriate nickname, The Yankee Clipper, with not only this style, but with a quality of leadership and sense of strength that seemed as natural as they were inimitable. "Have faith in the Yankees my son," Santiago tells the boy, "Think of the great DiMaggio." And the faithful were rewarded, for the Yankees led by DiMaggio won ten pennants and nine World Series. Clearly, DiMaggio and his Yankees were Something To Believe In, something solid, dependable, trustworthy, safe, secure, sacred. In 1941 DiMaggio hit safely in 56 consecutive games; he was a rock of consistency and dependability in an exploding world. And the image never faded. When he realized that he was slipping in 1951, DiMaggio promptly retired, his pride and dignity uncompromised and intact.

If Joe DiMaggio was the symbol of confident and successful leadership in the late Depression and again in the postwar splurge, then Ted Williams was the antithesis, the irresponsible isolationist. Not even Gionfriddo could destroy DiMaggio's poise and self-discipline; any garbage-mouth in the stands could incite Williams' temper. In 1941 Williams batted .406, but his team lost the pennant to DiMaggio's Yankees. Santiago does not recommend Williams to the boy, for loafing in the outfield and on the bases does not create faith. Williams was, in short, a threat to security, a Kid, an anti-hero.

Time mellowed Williams, however, and injuries threatened his career. Long after his shooting the pigeons in Fenway Park, he was recalled to active duty in Korea and nearly shot down himself. His return to baseball was widely hailed. Then in 1957 Williams had a memorable confrontation with DiMaggio's heir, Mickey Mantle. Mantle hit .365 and the 39 year-old Kid hit .388. Baseball fans finally accorded Williams the adulation he had always scorned and the recognition he had always deserved. With characteristic nostalgia they romanticized him as the last of the 400 hitters, the only man ever to hit

a Rip Sewell blooper out of sight, the greatest natural hitter since
Shoeless Joe Jackson. And Williams, though he never did tip his hat,
did not disappoint his fans at the plate. With his last swing he hit one
that, as John Updike wrote, was "in the books while it was still in
the sky." An anti-hero in the DiMaggio Era, Williams suffered hard
enough and settled down far enough to become the Artist in Residence,
the Compleat Batter, the Elder Sports Statesman of the Eisenhower
fifties.

Although Williams and DiMaggio became the predominant figures
in America's dominant sport in the late 30's, several other athletes received tremendous popular acclaim at that time. A young Bob Feller
captured America's eye, and a dying Lou Gehrig broke her heart.
Jesse Owens ran free in the stadium that Adolph Hitler policed, while
Tom Harmon ran wild in those that Red Grange built. Then the War.
In America's second favorite sport, college football, a Mr. Inside and
a Mr. Outside at West Point ran for daylight and for Old Glory. Pro-
moted by a chauvinistic press and magnified by bubblegum opposition,
Davis and Blanchard are the classic examples of heroes created to meet
the emotional needs of the times. If, as Frederick Lewis Allen has
suggested, Charles Lindbergh was deified by the "spiritually starved"
people of the Twenties, then Davis and Blanchard were lionized by the
patriotically charged people of the Duration.

Though not as riotous perhaps as the 20's that Johnny came
marching home to, the American scene that the ubiquitous Kilroy
re-entered was eager to replace the idols of war with the idols of
leisure. In this fast and exciting time there appeared one of the
fastest and most exciting players of all time—Jackie Robinson.

In his autobiography *The Way It Is,* Curt Flood describes how
"choked up" he felt when in 1970 Jackie Robinson testified on his
behalf before the U.S. District Court. This incident dramatizes the
emotional impact that Jackie Robinson has had on the black experience
in America. Historically, Jackie Robinson changed the nature of professional athletics, redirected the whole course of major league baseball,
and it is difficult, if not impossible, to overestimate the significance
of this fact. But in a personal sense Jackie Robinson gave black people
something they never had, not even from Joe Louis: a hero who was
not only better than the white man in the white man's game, but one
more intelligent than the white, and yet one proud to be black. Jack
Orr has described how the black people who flocked to Ebbetts Field

would react to Robinson's stealing second or spearing a line drive: "The faces would light up and take on a look of such undiluted bliss, of such bursting pride, that a stranger looking on might have imagined he was in a church."

Jackie Robinson was not, of course, a hero in the same universal sense as Joe Louis. Robinson's appeal was almost exclusively to black people, and it was counterpointed, if not overwhelmed, by a racist hostility unsurpassed in modern sports. "Opposing bench jockeys," as Roger Kahn details in *The Boys of Summer*, "forever shouted 'black bastard,' 'nigger lover,' and 'monkey-fucker;' " the old Dodger hero, Dixie Walker, demanded to be traded; and white fans everywhere vented their venom. Joe Louis was patronized by whites, Robinson incensed them. Historically, Joe Louis is the founding father of the Uncle Tom line of black athlete: Willie Mays, Henry Aaron, Elston Howard, Floyd Patterson, Arthur Ashe. Robinson spawned their alter black egos: Jimmy Brown, Bill Russell, Muhammed Ali, Kareem Jabbar, Tommy Smith, Curt Flood.

In a symbolic although sometimes real way, as with the Ali-Patterson fight, these two antithetical kinds of black hero have fought their own private battle over the last twenty years, a microcosm of the larger struggle around us. Today their battle is over. Floyd Patterson went down for a symbolic count, and Tommy Smith's gloved fist went up for a political gold medal. Willie Mays became a legend in the fifties by saying "Hey" and playing brilliantly. When in the seventies Willie responded to the Curt Flood suit against baseball's reserve clause by saying he would play anywhere if the paychecks were fat, he sounded as anachronistic as Disney's *Song of the South*, but proved as prophetic as Orwell's *1984*.

The gravestone of Tomism should be inscribed "Cassius Marcellus Clay." For as Eldridge Cleaver makes emphatically clear, Ali's punishing defeat of Patterson, the "bootlicking puppet," is both a "psychological chastisement of 'white' white America" and a political epiphany for the "faithful darkies, the embarrassed Uncle Toms" still surviving in the New World. Cleaver specifically alludes to Joe Louis as a puppet, a "fallen lion at every white man's feet;" Ali is the "first free black champion ever to confront white America." More recently, a white writer, Mark Kram, has identified Ali as the only American athlete today who has expressed the "temper and rhythm of his times to the point of becoming the embodiment of a social climate." Although this opinion overlooks, unfairly I believe, the significance of Joe Namath and Arnold Palmer, there is no challenging the judgment on Ali. As they did in Hobey Baker sixty years ago, athletic excellence, charismatic personality, and eponymous symbol crystallize in the figure and spirit of the once and, perhaps, Future King.

Politicization is clearly the central theme in the evolution of the black athlete as hero. Although not as dramatically manifested, this same theme does appear implicitly in the kinds of white athletic heroes who emerge in the Eisenhower Years. Mailer and Schlesinger both contend that there are no heroes in the fifties, but the emerging popularity of Mickey Mantle, Johnny Unitas, and Rocky Marciano plus the continuing appeal of Stan Musial suggests that the hero vacuum is more political than athletic. Where Musial appeals to the Boy Scout in all of us, each of the other three in his own distinctive way reflects the security, regularity, order, and small-townishness of the fifties which Mailer attacks.

Commerce, Oklahoma and Abilene, Kansas are geographical and spiritual neighbors. So in a way are their favorite sons, Mantle and Eisenhower. They are both just plain folk, simple, homespun, humble, unlettered, down-to-earth Okies from Muskogee. Mickey Mantle walked into the Yankees training camp in 1951 carrying a cardboard suitcase. He then proceeded to hit a baseball farther and to run to first base faster than anyone who had ever played the game. Some people thought that Krypton had struck again. Ironically, Mantle's awesome power and speed were generated by an engine that was intrinsically weak, osteomyelitis, and mechanically flawed, bad legs. Over the years Mantle's injuries unquestionably diminished his per-formance, but they tremendously enhanced his image as a hero. Even more than the tape-measure which he invented, Mantle became identified with the bandages, the hobble, the grimace, the pain. In Detroit, in Cleveland, in Boston, thousands came an hour early to see Mantle take batting practice, chorused him with the obligatory boos when he batted in the game, and then saluted him when he limped off for a pinch-runner in the late innings. Mickey Mantle did not, of course, fulfill the promise; he did not break Babe Ruth's record; The Wrong Man, the Anti-Hero of Baseball, Roger Maris did that. But Mantle, like all larger-than-life heroes, left a legacy: fans still point to that spot on the facade in Yankee Stadium, still recall the blood-soaked uniform in Pittsburgh, still wonder about the might-have-been.

If the image of Mickey Mantle comes close to the heart of the fifties, the other two outstanding heroes who emerged then, Rocky Marciano and Johnny Unitas, represent the soul and the mind of the times. Marciano is strength, innocence, simplicity, will, toughness, tenacity, humility; Unitas is skill, strategy, coolness, dexterity, precision, brinksmanship. It was impossible not to like the Rock, for even when he was destroying the Old King, Joe Louis, he was feeling sorry for him. Similarly, one had to admire Unitas, for he was able to do what every modern man dreams of doing—to control time by stopping the clock. As heroes, Marciano hearkens back to the primitive past while Unitas introduces the technological future. Marciano was quite literally the last of his kind, a white American heavyweight champion; while if in paradoxical fact, modern pro football was born in Sudden Death in 1958, then it was Unitas who performed the delivery.

Although not as close to Gandalf the Grey Wizard in age as George Blanda, Johnny Unitas is still playing in 1972. But like the pathetic Floyd Patterson and the wobbly Willie Mays who are also still competing, Johnny Unitas has been supplanted, superseded, deposed. The coup, which occurred on January 12, 1969, has been precisely interpreted by one of the participating revolutionaries, Johnny Sample:

> "We played a new kind of football and our heroes were a new
> breed of players. Men like Joe Namath who wore their hair
> long and bragged about how good they were had replaced the
> men like Johnny Unitas, the clean-cut All-American-kid type.

The Jets victory over the Colts in the '68 season Super Bowl was not an upset but a revolution, a burning down of the old order, the establishment National Football League, by the young turks, the American Football League. From the ashes of the Colt ruins sprang the avatar of the more supercool than brave new world, Joe Willie Namath.

Joe Willie Namath defines these times as sensationally as *The Godfather*, as controversially as Archie Bunker, as originally as Frank Zappa. From his Bachelors III Club to his Fu Manchu, from his Johnny Walker Red to his Persian Lamb coat, Joe Willie is the ultimate Playboy as Hero. In his autobiography, appropriately titled *I Can't Wait Until Tomorrow 'Cause I Get Better Looking Every Day,* Namath celebrates his own indulgence in tall blondes, booze, clothes, food, parties—in short, fun and freedom. Similarly, he cannot abide schedules, discipline,

authority, restraint, redheads, Pete Rozelle, and "bullshit." Icono-
clastic as he seems, Namath is, ironically, a hero in the classic epic
mold. For like Ali, Namath has unrestrained pride and self-confidence,
and in good epic fashion, he boasts of victory before the battle.
"We're going to win, I'll guarantee you," announced Joe Willie at the
Touchdown Club dinner before the Super Bowl. He was right.

Our age of polarization re-affirms Newton's Third Law: for
every Joe Namath there is an Arnold Palmer. Voted the Athlete of
the Decade by both the Associated Press and *Sports Illustrated*,
Palmer is the first genuine sports hero from a participant, as opposed
to spectator, sport. The popularity of Palmer not only points up the
direct effect that increased leisure time has had on our social history
but points to the continuous democratization of the old elitist sports.
For when Jack Dempsey was packing Boyle's Thirty Acres, Walter
Hagen was stroking knickered putts for the 400. Today we have
Arnie's Army, the first knot-hole gang in the history of golf, who, as
Frank Beard complains, "knock you down" to get near the King.
The choice of Palmer by the AP and *SI* is also revealing, politically
and psychologically. For almost everywhere Palmer is successful,
conservative, and, of course, white. He has not only charged to over
$1,000,000 earnings on the circuit but to corporate affluence and
White House friendship. In the '70 Greensboro Open, Palmer was
leading the field after the second round. As soon as he dropped his
last putt, he jumped into his own private jet, flew to Pennsylvania
to pick up his wife, and then dashed to a formal White House dinner.
Palmer flew back to Greensboro at 4:30 A.M. to play the final 36
holes. Naturally, he lost the tournament. But that's why he won the
awards.

Arnold Palmer may be the personification of the Middle American
Dream, the son of a teaching golf pro at a 9-hole course who plays
political Nassaus with Spiro Agnew and Bob Hope. But this identification with the reactionary *status quo* should not obscure the fact
that Arnold Palmer became golf's first superstar primarily because of
his electrifying style of play. Den Jenkins has graphically described
this style and its effect on all of us:

> Perhaps never again will there be a golfer with the universal
> appeal of Arnold Palmer. For more than a decade he has been
> a classic hero: bold, reckless, even foolhardy—traits that have
> cost him titles at times but have won him the admiration of

the world. Who cares if the shot must go under a limb yet
carry the pond? Go for it. Charge! On the tee he hammers
at the ball the same way we do, straining to get every last
yard out of it. Then he strides down the fairway, hitching
at his pants, impatient to get on to the next shot. On the
greens he agonizes over his putts and when they drop, his
joy is unrestrained.

This description of Palmer comes very close to defining the
archetype, the classic American sports here. For each of the
individuals discussed here, from Hobey Baker to Arnold Palmer, has
personified these same qualities: a passion for winning but a joy in
playing; a reckless, gambling style but a highly successful record; a
transcendent talent but a down-to-earth appeal.

Two athletes, Jack Nicklaus and Henry Aaron, provide empirical proof that each of these characteristics is required. Nicklaus is
now widely recognized as the greatest golfer ever to play the game—
the last unbeliever was blown into the Pacific from the 17th at the
Pebble. Yet Nicklaus will never have the appeal of Palmer. The
Bear doesn't "charge"; he doesn't have to. He is a relentless, ever-
powering perfectionist, a master technician, a *deus ex machina*. And
while Nicklaus has been running down the major titles record of
Bobby Jones, Hank Aaron has been closing in on Babe Ruth with
awesome inexorability. But for all the acclaim that he has received
in the last few years, Hank Aaron is simply not a folk hero, not a
Ruth nor a Willie Mays. Hank Aaron's 715th homer will be a
mausoleum not to brilliance but to endurance.

Who will be the heroes of tomorrow? Roger Staubach, Jim
Plunkett or O. J. Simpson? Vida Blue, Dave Kingman or Johnny
Bench? Can we predict where we're going from where we have
already been?

Future Shock notwithstanding, these predictions seem in
order: the heroes of the 70's will most likely be extremely talented,
exciting males—colorless perfectionists and women need not apply.
These heroes will have to sustain their talent, they will have to
endure, for fleeting brilliance, as that of Sandy Koufax and Gale
Sayers, might dazzle the eye but it does not grasp the heart. The
medium of television will increasingly deliver its cool McLuhanesque
message, diminishing the popularity of baseball and enhancing that
of football and hockey. Similarly, the Press will play an ever-expand-

ing role in the creation of heroes, and the widespread hostility of
the Press toward the baseball players strike suggests the direction it
might take. All athletes will become—if they are not already—polit-
icized; Dave Meggysey could conceivably make a comeback. Finally,
the democratization of sports will continue. Falconry may not
return but tennis could explode. Pancho Gonzales appeared twenty
years too soon, so that today the game desperately needs an
"Arnold Palmer." Certainly no one thought fifty years ago that
those elitist knickers would increase, multiply, and transmogrify into
vermillion bellbottoms for the weekend golfing masses. Who knows,
Bill Tilden's long drawers might suffer the same happy democratic
fate.

One final prediction: in the none too objective opinion of
this close-to-Boston observer there is one professional athlete today
who has already confirmed his reservation in the pantheon—Bobby
Orr. His performance against the Rangers in the Stanley Cup finals
was consummate. The daring fake-out of Bruce MacGregor to score,
the pass to Bucyk, and the tyrannizing control of the puck against the
Rangers strong power play represent levels of offensive and defensive
excellence that in an increasingly specialized athletic world are
extraordinarily rare. And all this on a knee awaiting surgery.

Does Bobby Orr have the personality, the magnetism, to
complement his skill, and can a Canadian citizen playing a carpetbag-
ger sport become a national hero in the United States? Speaking for
every hockey fan in America who has tried to get tickets to a Bruins
game, for every father in suburbia who has discovered the fireplace
screen in the middle of the street, for every mother in the inner city
who has cooked a 3:30 A.M. breakfast, I'll say "Hell, yes." And
when those kids start raising street-hockey dust storms in Atlanta,
Georgia and Long Island next year, then everyone will know the
truth of the bumper-sticker plastered to the unused backboard on
my garage: THIS IS ORR COUNTRY.

NOTES

1In his *Franklin Roosevelt and The New Deal,* William E. Leuchtenburg points out that in the thirties, so much emphasis is given to social security and collective action that the America that hailed the Lone Eagle criticizes Amelia Earhart for her irresponsible exploit.

2c Ted Carroll, "The Black Man in Boxing," *Ring* XLVIII (December, 1969), p. 46.

3Carroll, p. 46.

R. Charnigo

By RONALD CUMMINGS
The Superbowl Society

Heroism is a product of history and cultural context as well as
psychological need. Joseph Campbell's "hero with a thousand faces"
is strikingly singular in pattern but splendidly complex and diverse
in particular manifestations. The various incarnations of the heroic
design of separation-initiation-return are significant indices of central
preoccupations of specific cultural environments.

America has gone through many heroes. Marshall Fishwick and
Dixon Wecter have chronicled their history demonstrating the evolution of American mythic configuration. Our heroic heritage is similar
to the artistic heritage described by T. S. Eliot in "Tradition and the
Individual Talent": each adopted hero contributes to the cultural
construct, reinforcing it and altering it in some meaningful way. Our
heroes change because our perception of reality changes, although
once we have created a hero he lingers on influentially in historical
perspective. We do not abandon heroes, merely create new contexts
for them in the very process of our living beyond them. A contemporary example of a shift in heroic role is that of the Indian and pioneer.
The former is becoming less a figure of pure evil and savagery and more
a figure of primitive goodness, simplicity, and courage. The slaughter-
ing white is now coming to be viewed as the barbarian. Involved in this

transformation is the entire spectrum of American myth and its
reflection of a dominant national conflict between an unspoiled
natural order and an encroaching civilization. In our own complex
time when the social order seems particularly confusing and confin-
ing, the life of the noble Indian is especially appealing. And in a
culture which has established itself by fiat disguised in the vestments
of divine destiny (and which continues to assert itself by such means
in Southeast Asia), the burden of guilt must be expiated, the injustice
purged. The recent rise of the black hero denotes a similar concern
with social inequity which is at once altering and being assimilated
by the mythological structure.

Moreover, the continual dialectic between father and son, old
and young, king and subject, the oppressor and the oppressed is sub-
merged in the Indian/pioneer, black/white, hippie/cop dichotomies.
Seasonally the vegetation god must be decapitated; annually the babe
must supplant the tired old man. The heroic design is necessarily
one of death and renewal, of established order and agitation for
change, of authority and rebellion. One essential part of Americans
has always rejected the authority figure of civilization (Freud, of
course, delineated the opposition of the ego and society in his *Civilization and Its Discontents*). From the founding escapees of America
to Roger Williams to Natty Bumppo to Huck Finn, we have continually "lit out for the territory," for the expansive, free West, the camping grounds, the commune, Haight Ashbury, Woodstock; each generation re-learning that escape is impossible. (The present generation is
painfully discovering, the earthly territory gone, that despite their
discovery of inner space through drugs and ancient oriental and Christian mysticism, and outer space through technology, the imperative
of return and acceptance remains.)

We identify with the rebel as well as the establishment; they are
dual aspects of our sense of the need for reform and the need for
order. Our struggle is to reconcile the opposites, and historically
our efforts have been cyclical. In my own lifetime, for instance,
the country chose a benign father figure as President in the fifties.
In the sixties it chose a symbol of youth and "vigor" and had another
father figure thrust upon it instead which it could not accept. In the
early seventies we seem to be returning to the mood of the fifties, a
withdrawal from upheaval and violence, from rebellion, in quest of

a restored order. A creeping nostalgia is about and the sixties do, indeed, see that past as a distant country.

Our mythic structure, then, the mythic structure of any people, is inclusive; it must accommodate all of our conflicting, paradoxical desires. It is, after all, the primary embodiment of our most essential selves, both individually and nationally. We have our rebels from the Salem witches to the Chicago Seven, and our authority figures from the "father of our country" to LBJ. And within that range of possibilities we can somewhere gauge ourselves.

I have thought it unwise to take on singlehandedly all of our American heroes, and I will limit myself here to three contemporary figures from a particular segment of our culture. We draw our heroes from all corners of our lives; the corner I have chosen to investigate here is sport. The realm of sport has traditionally, since its post-civil war rise to eminence, provided us with heroes because it is itself a metaphorical world of masculine conflict simulating human endeavors to strive and triumph. The essential aspects of American sport are basic expressions of the American cultural pattern. To paraphrase Marshall McLuhan, the medium of sport is also the message. The very forms of our sport indicate dominant temporal and spatial national features. If the hunt was the central expression of sport in pre-industrial, state-of-nature America with its expansive landscape and assertion of a primal relationship between man and nature, then baseball, football, basketball and the like are the central expressions of an urban, technological, electronic America reflecting its concern with social structure and interpersonal relationships. Our literature has long lamented the passing of the frontier. Hemingway's work, in one sense, is a culmination of regrets. In a world of increasing complexity, restriction, sprawling bureaucracy, huge metropolitan areas and corporations, we have few spatial escapes remaining. The old frontier is gone; the "new frontier" is a dubious future. The suburbs are another type of confinement and the camping grounds too are crowded. Our national parks, our game and fish preserves are further efforts to retain and contain nature. Since industrial America severed work from a sense of fulfillment, we have turned more and more to sport as an accessible means of self-completion. This is the reason for the cheer and sense of release when the batter sends the ball soaring out of the park; the pleasure of the stuff shot, the breakaway; the satisfaction of the bomb, the punt return, the long gainer. Our modern sports are attempts to break out of an artificially imposed confinement. Curt Gowdy's "American Sportsman" is a staged idyll; the Sunday afternoon pro football game a social reality. Nature has disappeared from most contemporary lives, shut out by gigantic buildings, train and walkway tunnels, a densely populated atmosphere. We have restructured our environment and our relations to it, and the artificial turf and Astrodome are physical symbols in the sport realm, a realm which has historically been associated with the "outdoorsman."

American sport, like American culture in general, has its origins in Europe and specifically in England. Our artists have lived with that Old World burden and the challenge to scratch out a new tradition on what has often seemed poor tenant soil. But the very attempt to import and adapt has always wrought original transformations despite feelings of imitative inferiority.[1] The adoption and adaptation of ancient forms of sport and the diffusion from the upperclass to the wider population offer insight into a social order's composition and preoccupations.[2] In America golf, football, and baseball all begin with the concept of exclusiveness and clubs. Golf is an overt vestige of the pastoral European upperclass sporting code. Baseball, a game we like to claim as our own invention but which has direct ties with ancient ball games, cricket, and the English children's rounders,[3] combines the expansive sense of the pastoral leisure of golf with a high degree of organization and cooperative structure. It is at once a reflection of a more interdependent social order and an urban containment of the natural environment. Football, too, manifests these same two elements, and its open conflict and violence, speed and simultaneous action project both fundamental aggressive aspects of the American character embedded deep in the Puritan sensibility, the hostility of colonial nature, and frontier existence, and a more explicit urban tempo. Unlike golf which merely uses the landscape, baseball and football corral the pastoral and mirror man's triumph over his natural setting, his containment and dominance of nature which is at once his triumph and his predicament. Basketball, despite its peach basket origin and the barnyard hoops of Indiana, was city born (in a YMCA) and, completely enclosed, represents the urban in its pace and design. Ice hockey also has this urban impulse, while boxing, like wrestling, with its small ring and one-to-one elemental conflict has always been a less localized metaphor for human strife. Basically lower class, the formalization of the fight has moved from a rural to an urban geography without significant change except that the "asphalt jungle" has colored it with racial overtones.

Clearly, then, though I will not trace the patterns further, the form of sport alone suggests a cultural configuration. Moreover, sport provides metaphorical insight into the fundamental ritualistic and mythological framework of a society. Gregory Stone in a *Chicago Review* article in 1955 discusses the substance of sport as play and dis-play, the latter being the element of spectacle and pageantry.[4] Historically, sport has been related to religious rites and festivals, as P. C. McIntosh has indicated in his *Sport in Society*.[5] Robert Henderson in his *Ball, Bat and Bishop* traces all ball and bat games to ancient fertility rite origins. The reason for the seemingly wide disparity between sport and religion in modern society is found in the movement of civilization from a primitive, unified vision of reality to a dispersed, increasingly fragmented one, the continuing separation and departmentalization of roles and functions resulting in extreme specialization. Thus, although Veblen contends that initially sport and religion arise from the same fundamental "belief in an inscrutable propensity or a preternatural interposition in the sequence of events" (*TLC*, p. 295), they seem strange bedfellows in our society.

Yet in contemporary American culture there remains a curious connection between our religious and, in a more and more secularized world, our national holidays. New Year's Day has long been a football festival with the most lavish pageantry. The Rose Bowl parade is a most unusual display of the American Adam's garden, a motorized nature division. The other bowl games have varying degrees of elaborate pre-game spectacles, and on that day of days, the bowl games may be viewed from dawn until dawn, ushering in the year. Some not-so-far-distant connection with fertility and national vitality must be admitted in all of this. Our Thanksgiving Day parades are more commercial in nature, culminating in the arrival of the patron saint of getting and spending, Santa Claus. And that sacred Puritan holiday is rapidly becoming one of post-feasting football. Christmas, our most revered religious holiday, is fraught with basketball tournaments, and I venture to surmise that it is not the sanctity of the season which explains the absence of football but the proximity of the New Year spectacle. Independence Day is traditionally associated with picnics and baseball as well as stupendous fireworks displays which are, indeed, national orgasms of a sort. Since religious pageantry has waned, due in part to an original Puritan influence and to the secularization of society, sport has become increasingly a function for such display. Super Sunday may soon be our most gala affair of all. The most recent Super Bowl celebration was a microcosmic view of America of macrocosmic proportions complete with a pre-game military exhibition and a halftime show featuring Al Hirt and Ella Fitzgerald, and young players-to-be, pre-initiates competing in a national punt and pass contest. Perhaps one of the reasons football seems to be replacing baseball as America's national sport is because of its incorporation of such pageantry.

This spectacular ceremonial feature of sport is combined with an elementary symbolic portrayal. Because the realm of sport is one of play, pretend, fantasy (to the point that we cease caring that it is staged and accept the roller derby and professional wrestling as our modern morality plays), it contains the mythological framework of the culture in miniature. Time is compressed and relatively clearcut patterns emerge. Sport involves the rather naive elements of children's allegory. My folk heroes were Superman, the Lone Ranger, and Pinkie Lee. My son's seem to be Big Bird, the Bugaloos, and Mr. Rogers. I idolized Norm VanBrocklin, Bob Davies (the blonde streak of the NBA in its days of crackerbox gyms and white supremacy); Arnold Palmer, Cassius Clay/Muhammad Ali, and Willie Joe Namath seem to be three current sport idols and, like mine, they possess broad mythic implications.

Arnold Palmer is, to borrow a phrase, "the great white hope," a representative of the Protestant, middleclass myth of the wholesome, clean-living, dedicated, fair-haired all-American boy who succeeds with flair, grace, determination, and humility. His squint down the fairway, head cocked to one side, is as symbolic as his hurried charge to the ball when his game is right. His style, as Jim Murray has pointed out in his column, is that of hitting through rather than along the dogleg, of refusing to play it safe, of dreaming the impossible dream, making the impossible shot: ". . . facing up to challenge or even relishing a challenge—is what sport is all about. . . . The real pleasure is in pulling off the impossible."[6]

Moreover, Palmer is a gentleman in a gentleman's game. Golf itself is the sport of the great white hope. It is a game of status, of the country club, of suburbia and high fashion. It clings to the pastoral myth as well as the mythic code of clean-living, a code which is one of upper class self-justification imported from Europe. As Veblen observed, originally sporting is what one did instead of work; it was a "conspicuous" sign of superiority. In America sport was maligned by the Puritans as a sensuous distraction from the spiritual. Play, as Gregory Stone indicates, had to be linked with work in order for it to be accepted as legitimate activity. As America evolved from a society of producers to one of consumers, the roles of work and play were fused. One result is professional athletics.

Despite its astounding financial rewards (indeed, in this day of economic status, because of them) the image of golf has remained one of Old World favor with its gentleman ideal. It retains the mythic figure of Gilbert Patten's Frank Merriwell stories, of an athletic ideal that is also a social ideal. This image has pervaded, to some extent, all sport, but is one which has been and continues to be dispelled, initially by Ring Lardner and Mark Harris, and subsequently by a flood of exposé and inside stories. Nevertheless, golf remains relatively unscathed. The myth hangs on in Arnold Palmer, who is himself hanging on. That Palmer is fading from the contemporary golf scene hardly matters, however; his legend is already reality. I could have as easily used Jack Nicklaus as a symbolic figure here, or almost any other current player with the exceptions of Lee Trevino and Dave Hill (the Chicano and bad boy of the circuit). I could even have used Charlie Sifford, one of golf's few blacks. Or, I could have used John Unitas, or Brooks Robinson. Young Bob Griese, who claims he leads by example, is the single young sport participant who occurs to me. The others are approaching retirement. I doubt, however, that the myth will join them although it seems of a bygone era. How long will eternal George Blanda play? Myths die (if they ever do) hard. It is more exact to suggest the protean nature of mythic fabric, the continually evolving, shifting context. To take the disappearance of Johnny U's flattop as some essential change is to be utterly deceived.

If Palmer is the old white hope, Cassius Clay/Muhammad Ali (an intriguing dual personality) is the new black hope. His symbolic dimensions have been delineated by Eldridge Cleaver in his discussion of the Clay/Patterson fight in *Soul on Ice*, and more recently by Norman Mailer. He is a focal point of the new black identity, the athlete "black militant" (a new white euphemism for "uppity

nigger"). Mailer contends that "he is America's greatest Ego."
There is a real irony in making that claim of any black man in this
country. The current seemingly excessive black ego, the hostility
and defensiveness, is merely another effort to survive, to assert
self-integrity. Exaggeration is a compensation for insecurity. Excessive ego is a natural progression from non-ego. We protect ourselves with submission and humility when we must; we speak our
outrages when we can.

We have embarked upon a new period of race relations in
America and Ali already embodies its myth along with Malcolm
X, Cleaver, George Jackson, Fred Hampton, and Angela Davis. The
current Ali is not, of course, Cassius Clay. He has become more
acceptable to white society. But it doesn't really matter now. The
point is that Ali was Clay, that he was brash and arrogant and
mouthy, that he wasn't your humble nigger, that he would spit in
your eye, and that he refused to be inducted into the armed service,
denied, on religious and ethical grounds, the American involvement
in Viet Nam. Clay was volatile and explosive. He was an embodiment of Detroit, Watts, and to cross racial lines, Chicago, and Kent
State. In addition, he was a supreme boxer; his fights emblematic.
Boxing is a black man's sport, a poor man's sport (though eventually
all the main sports of a consumer society become rites of passage
for the dis-possessed). Training comes in the streets. The ring is
especially symbolic for a black man; it not only expresses his experience in America of enslavement but it is an apparent opportunity
to retaliate. Only most often he has merely been in that grotesque
situation described so vividly at the outset of Ellison's *Invisible Man,*
beating his own image at his own expense for the gratification of
the honkies. Clay didn't merely defeat Patterson and Liston, he
defeated a white image of the black man; he mutilated a myth, a
myth that the myth of Arnold Palmer had thrust upon him. Whites,
consequently, were intimidated and loathed him. The Frazier victory (Frazier the huge, dark, ponderous black who sings and skips
rope to music on stage) was a return to normalcy, but deceptively
so. It is really only a superficial respite, no reprieve or reversal of
the decision. Ali represents a new black pride. Despite formal
action taken to strip him of his title, he remained, still remains, the
titular champion. Ask a young black who Ali is. Or recall that
meaningful post-Super Bowl interview between Dallas running back

Duane Thomas and nervous sportscaster Tom Brookshire. If Palmer
and Unitas are near retirement, Ali is making a comeback. Howard
Cossell, for once, is right; Ali is different. So are we.

In the midst of it all, between Palmer and Ali somewhere, is
a product of that collegiate "Papa Bear," strict authoritarian father
figure Paul Bryant, Joe Willie Namath. Boyish, naive, shy, he was
apparently as innocent as the American Adam, a regular teddy bear,
when he first broke into the AFL. Indeed, his progress in professional
football is in the tradition of the American loss of innocence from
Arthur Mervyn to Huck Finn to Holden Caulfield. He has been the
"hippie" of the sport world, the boy who came from a small town
in Pennsylvania to the big city, became a star, was tainted, rebelled,
and was disillusioned. He is the mythic youth of the sixties, a
symbolic figure of student unrest, of the mod style, of another type
of arrogance, not as offensive to Americans as Clay's, but a type
they admire—a kind of egotistical assurance. Believe anything,
everything. Most of all, believe in yourself and your own ability.
America is a land of promises and dreams come true, of log cabins
to presidents, of lowly New York Jets to Super Bowls. Namath is
a sport type of the new American breed of kids who once again
took that mystical journey west in quest of El Dorado and found
Haight Ashbury instead, of a vociferous rejection of middle class
hypocrisy, of an attempt to actually live middle class morality,
and most of all, of disenchantment. His sojourn is a replica of the
decade's youth cult: the outward manifestation of rebellion in
hair style and clothing; the disputes with the commissioner about
his life style and the implications that he was ruining the image of
professional football; rumours of his permissive, bachelor life which
his nightclub seemed to corroborate. Joe Willie was a combination
of an idealistic view of personal freedom and individuality and,
ironically, the male vision of Hugh Heffner. Every male in the
country had penis envy; every female had hot pants before they
were in *Vogue*.

And who was Joe Willie Namath, anyhow? Who were all
those kids at Washington demonstrating against the war, campaigning for Clean Gene, at Woodstock, at Kent State? Joe Willie was
American innocence and idealism equipped with nothing more than
the myth of Arnold Palmer. You can come from twenty strokes
back and win on the last hole. You can win the Super Bowl with

a last place team. You can conquer racism, war and poverty. You can purge evil from the world. You can be free. And then, the all-American thud, the crying outside the commissioner's office, saying how much he loved football; the assassinations, Kent State, the bombing at Wisconsin. *Easy Rider,* despite or because of its flaws, is the parable of the decade, of such "easy" idealism and its consequences, as well as another in a long line of artistic repetitions of this American dilemma. We are still very much Puritans at heart. Joe Willie is another of our symbolic heroes, complete with mythic wound (his injured knee), stretching back to the Separatists who left England because it was not pure enough, to Seeker Roger Williams who left the Puritans because they were not pure enough (Perry Miller has shown that it wasn't a matter of religious toleration in any democratic sense at all), to Anne Hutchinson, and the witches of Salem, to Hawthorne and Melville and on and on. Bernard Malamud has mythologized the process in a sport framework in *The Natural.* Americans continue to emerge from the virgin woods and lose their manheads.

Leslie Fiedler contended at the last MLA convention that we have just come through a cultural revolution. Maybe so. But it is surely a continuing process, and though we already seem somewhere beyond the very myths I have suggested here, we are also still mired in them up to our infamous bootstraps. There is always the fear of that terrible quicksand nightmare: that the harder we struggle to climb out, the deeper we sink. We must be careful that we do not exclude any means of spotting the quagmires or the configurations which contain them—even in such unlikely places as green the ring, and the football field.

NOTES

[1] See David Riesman and Reuel Denny, "Football in America: A Study in Culture Diffusion," *American Quarterly,* 3, (1951), 309-319.

[2] Thorstein Veblen's *The Theory of the Leisure Class* (New York: Vanguard Press, 1899) is still a provocative study of the elitist origin of sport. For American sport in particular see Robert H. Boyle's *Sport—Mirror of American Life* (Boston: Little, Brown and Co., 1963). Boyle comments: "American sport is not of the people, the frontier, but upper class and urban in impulse" (p. 5).

[3] See Robert Henderson, *Ball, Bat and Bishop* (New York: Rockport Press, 1947).

[4]Gregory F. Stone, "American Sports: Play and Dis-Play," *Chicago Review*, 9 (Fall 1955), 83-100.

[5](London: C. A. Watts & Co., 1968), pp. 23-24.

[6]Arnold Palmer, "Joys of Trouble," *Sports Illustrated*, 26 July 1965, pp. 34-38.

By ANTHONY HOPKINS
Contemporary Heroism — Vitality in Defeat

I wish to describe a pattern for the presentation of the nature, predicament and fate of the hero as it appears in a number of contemporary novels and films. The pattern appears frequently (approximately thirty-six examples have turned up so far) and it appears with a high degree of consistency, not only among obviously similar works such as *Catch-22* and *One Flew Over the Cuckoo's Nest,* but also works of apparently intense diversity such as *The First Circle, Butch Cassidy and the Sundance Kid,* and *Scandalous John.* It dominates *The Anderson Tapes* and *If* in different ways, significantly informs *Midnight Cowboy, Easy Rider, Bonnie and Clyde.*

It reflects, I will suggest, a widely perceived and deeply felt sense of the nature and of the predicament of ordinary people in the modern world.

The major features of the pattern of heroism are:

1. *The hero possesses exceptional natural vitality,* both in terms of masculine energy and spiritual integrity; perhaps coupled with spontaneous charity and humanity. In any case, his virtues are native rather than civilized, tending toward potency rather than purity, cunning rather than honour.

2. *Society is inherently and massively repressive,* by its

113

nature and in its operations opposed to vitality, eccentricity, individuality, independence.

3. *Despite increasing social pressure, the hero remains nonconforming.* The hero—who possesses neither social power nor influence—stands alone in essential spiritual opposition to social forces encroaching ever more progressively upon his independence and freedom.

4. *The hero suffers defeat, destruction, death.*

The dimensions of the natural vitality possessed by the hero are perhaps most consciously articulated by Joseph Heller, when he has Yossarian give this opinion of himself in *Catch-22:*

> ". . . they couldn't touch him because he had a sound mind in a pure body and was as strong as an ox. They couldn't touch him because he was Tarzan, Mandrake, Flash Gordon. He was Bill Shakespeare. He was Cain, Ulysses, the Flying Dutchman; he was Lot in Sodom, Deidre of the Sorrows, Sweeny in the nightingales among the trees. He was miracle ingredient Z-247. He was—'—immense. I'm a real, slam-bang, honest-to-goodness, three-fisted humdinger. I'm a bona fide supraman.' " At the end of the novel he searches for Nately's whore's kid sister to rescue her and take her with him on his escape to Sweden.

But essentially the same intense impulse toward life characterizes other heroes such as:

> McMurphy of *Cuckoo's Nest,* former logger and general hell-raiser, described by one of the mental hospital doctors as "a Napoleon, Genghis Khan, Attila the Hun." McMurphy cheats constantly, swears floridly, flouts all the hospital rules, and reduces ward routine to chaos, in the process, however, helping the patients win back confidence, self-respect, dignity.

> Scandalous John McAndless of the Disney movie *Scandalous John,* who, defending his decaying ranch from a real estate developer, shoots first, then puts on his glasses. John helped lots of ranchers in the valley in the past, but now, to raise mortgage payments, he takes his one longhorn on a "cattle drive," resolutely ignoring the freeways and skyscrapers in his way.

> Nerzhin, the prisoner-scientist in *The First Circle,* bent both on creating the illusion of industrious research on a telephone voice-identification attachment and on attempting to seduce the female MGB agent who works in the lab.

> Joe Buck, of *Midnight Cowboy,* who supplies perhaps the
> ultimate affirmation of the superiority of raw, vital, human
> energy over any socially accepted mode of controlled be-
> haviour: "Ah ain't no real cowboy, but Ah am one hell of
> a stud."

The precise combination of physical and ethical qualities varies, but what does not vary is the principle of vitality. In this respect the outlaw, the psychopath, the coward, the barbarian are all one: their energy, creative or demonic, is totally opposed, as energy, to social conformity, inertia, stagnation, repression.

The nature of the basic social situation in which the hero is placed—a situation characterized by immersion, alienation, oppression —may be well illustrated through reference to the world of the boys' public (i.e. private) school depicted in *If.* At "College," the environment surrounding the boys has the principal effect of breaking youthful spirit and vitality. Through fear and punishment the boys are coerced into introjecting willing conformity to social ideals and practices which are shown, to the audience, to be hypocritical, perverted, inhumane.

Among the boys a rigid hierarchy of totalitarian authority prevails, the very youngest serving as "Scum"—personal servants—to the seniors, the "Whips," who sport military swagger sticks and maintain discipline on behalf of the masters. At one point in the film the Whips savagely cane the hero for having an "insolent manner" displeasing to them. The company of girls is strictly forbidden, but homosexuality is tolerated. Religious services are both daily and compulsory, as is service in the Army cadet corps, both activities being directed by the chaplain. The headmaster mouths platitudes of progressive education and social responsibility, but the traditions of pedogogical sterility, physical abuse, and aristocratic snobbery remain unaltered.

It is against such a world that the hero Mick—who drinks Vodka, plays records of Zulu war chants, initiates his friends into blood—brotherhood—revolts. On awards day, he, some few chums, and a girl friend, begin shooting up the assembly with old smoke bombs, hand grenades, mortars and machine guns they found in the auditorium basement. But the parents, guests and masters get guns and ammunition from the school armoury. Then, led by the guest of honour—a general —and with considerable energy and real hatred, they begin shooting back. The film ends with Mick, a Tommy-gun on his hip, firing, firing into the steadily advancing forces of the parental establishment.

Additionally instructive with respect to the nature of society is the totally police-state atmosphere of *The First Circle.* Solzhenitsyn's consistent metaphor for Soviet society is the prison, the least repressive and the least hellish of which is the laboratory-prison for scientists and technicians where Nerzhin is lodged. Unlike many of the apartments and dormitories in Moscow it has enough heat, reliable electricity, plentiful food; and those inside are reasonably certain about their status in the eyes of the authorities and the many varieties of police.

Also, the novel emphasizes, both prisoners and citizens are probably better off than Stalin, depicted as an impotent old man living in an essential prison—a guarded apartment inside a guarded fortress—for fear of treachery, including treachery from the secret police. The system of harassment, reprisal, repression, the state of constant suspicion and instant arrest, has become so thoroughly entrenched at all levels of Soviet government and society that it operates beyond anyone's effective control.

The heroic life force and society's prison-like and repressive sterility exist, initially, in a condition of polar incompatibility from which the conflicts and actions of the novels and films proceed. In most cases, the plot depicts the progressive, implacable encroachment of powerful social forces upon the more vital, but socially powerless hero.

Butch and Sundance, faced with thicker safes, armed bank guards, fancy alarm systems, and organized, relentless pursuit, light out for supposedly greener fields. But no matter how fast, how far they run, the straw-hatted railroad detective follows, first through the Wyoming rangeland, then through Bolivian jungles.

In *The Anderson Tapes,* the medium of encroachment is technological surveillance. Duke Anderson, just released from ten years in prison, immediately begins to promote and arrange his next job: robbing an entire apartment building. However, almost everywhere he goes someone or something is listening, watching, recording, photographing—jails, bus stations, banks, cars, beds, telephones, olives, neckties—everything has a lens or a mike attached. In the end, many groups of investigators, government and private, have information on Duke, on his innocent public actions, his criminal conspiracies, his sexual intimacies.

Yossarian, surrounded by the Air Force and by Catch-22, malingers in hospital, sabotages missions. Convinced everyone is trying to kill him, he begins walking backward to keep from getting jumped from behind. In the mental hospital, McMurphy suffers the straight-jacket, then shock therapy, then a lobotomy.

The outcome of this process of pressure and encroachment is, almost without exception, the total defeat, usually the death of the hero.

At the very best, there is a possibility of a personal escape that does nothing, however, to alter the basic conditions of society. Yossarian runs toward Sweden, but with no guarantee that he gets there. The Florida Joe Buck finally gets to in *Midnight Cowboy* is not so very different from the Texas he initially runs from. In *Cuckoo's Nest* the Indian, Chief Bromden, escapes from the asylum after ritually killing his god McMurphy, but his tribe's ancestral fishing grounds, where he intends to go, are owned by the U.S. government, which has put a dam across the river.

Occasionally, although defeated, the hero is not killed. At the conclusion of *The First Circle,* Nerzhin is being transferred from the prison for scientists to the very centre of Soviet hell—a forced labour camp in Siberia.

More typically, however, the conclusion of the unequal struggle between individual vitality and social organization is portrayed through the physical death of the hero, usually in terms that are violent and shocking, and by means that are either socially acceptable or officially sanctioned.

Old John McAndless is shot by an employee protecting his land-developer master from the possibility of assault from the semi-senile old man. McMurphy is lobotomized, basically, because he is incorrigible, not because he is insane. In *Easy Rider,* Wyatt and Billy get potted by a Louisiana redneck because they ride motorcycles and the guns are in the cab of the pickup truck anyhow. Bonnie Parker and Clyde Barrow are ambushed, in grisly slow motion, by a squad of deputies firing Thompson sub-machine guns. Duke Anderson is overrun by an assault from the New York City infantry battalion known as the Tactical Police, and Butch and Sundance charge into the concentrated rifle fire of a company of Bolivian cavalry.

These are executions, characterized by gratuitous severity and indiscriminate inefficiency, for in all cases the firepower brought to bear upon the hero is far in excess of what might be reasonably needed to subdue him, far out of proportion to the offense committed.

Repeatedly, however, this fondness for overkill is represented as evidence of society's spiritual inertia rather than as proof of its ruth-less evil. The proposition seems to be that a well-organized, efficient syndicate of power-mongers, firm of purpose and in complete control, would neither encourage nor admire such massive overdoses of de-struction.

But the efficient elimination of the unconventional or the naturally humane is more characteristic of *Brave New World* or *1984*. In the present works, society appears, instead, to be an almost random accumulation of a mass of attitudes and practices tending toward the conservative, the torpid, the normal, the predictable. Amorphous and uncoordinated, society derives its power from its incredible mass and imponderable bulk. Like any primitive life form, once disturbed it reacts unconsciously, totally, to engulf and overwhelm the irritation. With the exception of Stalin, the highest official in any of the works is rarely above the ranks of middle management—a ward nurse, a subaltern officer, a sheriff. Society has no rulers, only servants.

Perhaps the most graphic illustration of the ungoverned yet inevitable victory of society is furnished by *The Anderson Tapes*. Duke and his gang are annihilated by the Tactical Police, but the cause of their downfall is almost accidental. In one of the apartments the gang finds a crippled boy. Thinking him helpless, they do not restrain him. The boy crawls to a short-wave transmitter he owns, begins broadcasting Mayday calls on a ham frequency. The random signals are monitored by ham operators who happen to be listening, and from all over the U.S. phone calls reporting the robbery come to the N.Y.P.D. switchboard.

The point, of course, is that none of the public agencies or private investigators who have information about Duke have any hand in his betrayal or killing. All have been working independently, often illegally, without knowledge of each other's activities, let alone access to one another's data. It is just that there is such a vast amount of electronic and technological hardware around and in operation that Duke is, anyhow in the end, trapped through electronic means.

With the above examples of wanton social repression, the final segments of the pattern projected at the beginning of the paper fall, I hope, demonstrably together. Certainly to my own satisfaction the configuration of alienated vitality, coercive social conformity, and the victory of social stability over exceptional individuality has been demonstrated as basically applicable to the works that have been discussed.

As suggested earlier, it is a pattern of basic similarity that transcends a range of diversities which would otherwise profoundly separate and distinguish the individual works one from the other.

It embraces a wide variety of artistic styles and forms, from the high individuality of Solzhenitsyn's moral realism and Heller's innovative excursions into a perpetual horror, to the G-rated technicolour catastrophes of the Disney organization. It also transcends boundaries of geography, culture, ideology. The Russian state, the English school, the American city are all equally condemned, in the same terms, as prisons, as repositories of institutionalized violence and repression all equally engaged in the process of destroying the unique individual sensibility.

The extent of the range of inclusiveness of the pattern is all the more impressive when one considers that, for example, it was quite unlikely that Heller and Solzhenitsyn were aware of each others work. In fact, as far as I know, it is the rule rather than the exception among the entire group of works from which the selection for this paper was made, that they were each conceived of, at least originally, as unique embodiments of independent visions of the condition of modern mankind.

But, considering the frequency with which this vision has been offered, and the sustained and widespread acceptance it has received, it would seem reasonable to suggest that it flourishes because it touches, significantly, a centre of sensibility common to literally millions of people, a core of feeling shared by Russian intellectuals making personal copies of *The First Circle,* high-riding teenagers watching *Easy Rider* for the third time, and curious professors buying both in paperback at a newsstand.

In the plight of the contemporary hero, it seems to me, people can see the essential fate of their own feelings of individuality and their own personal freedom. Duke is in the position of any entrepreneur trying to make inroads upon corporate solidarity; both Nerzhin and Yossarian are in a situation not significantly different from that of any man of spirit working for any large government organization. Butch and Sundance are being rendered obsolete by a stern new world they never made and cannot understand, and, unlike Huck Finn, they cannot escape to the frontier.

In the image of the annihilated hero, I would suggest, people see embodied and expressed their own real but perhaps inarticulate tension, anxiety, and sense of victimization at the hands of social pressures and institutions, inimicable toward individual action and personal satisfaction, over which neither they nor anyone else seems to have any degree of significant directional influence.

In these times it would seem that the powerful impact of *The First Circle* lies not in Solzhenitsyn's presentation of a state of Communist torture frightening because of its utter difference from the democratic experience, but because, on the basis of their own experience, his readers here (and everywhere) can appreciate the accuracy of his portrayal of pressure and fear as the common denominators of life within a society that is, simultaneously, totally organized and uncontrolled, devoid of purpose, yet ruthlessly engaged upon the elimination of human desires and designs from all human affairs.

Appendix: *The Jail and The Field*

In many of the works using the pattern of heroism outlined in the body of this essay it is frequently the case that the repressiveness of society crystallizes in the image and concept of the jail, the condition of natural human freedom and fulfillment through the sympathetic treatment of the open countryside.

As an example of a work in which this physical embodiment of spiritual opposition is used with illustrative effectiveness, one cannot do better than Edward Abbey's *The Brave Cowboy*, a work in which it is exploited with almost obsessive thoroughness.

The Brave Cowboy has essentially only two settings, each of which vies for symbolic dominance—the open range outside Duke City, New Mexico, and the interior of the county jail located inside Duke City. Significant portions of the book are given over to long, lyrical, yet restrained evocations of the healthy, independent, solitary, manly life of the free and open range—frying beans and bacon over a brushwood fire, listening to the birds, talking to the horse, looking off through clear air toward distant blue hills, stalking deer for jerky. The jail, into which the cowboy purposely contrives to get thrown, and from which he immediately begins to escape by filing through the bars, is dirty, smelly, boring, lifeless, debilitating. It contains persecuted Indians, a sadistic guard, stupid deputies, and a paunchy, lethargic politically corrupted sheriff. The last third of the novel chronicles the pursuit of the cowboy by a sheriff's posse of squad cars, a jeep, local volunteers, an Indian tracker, an Air Force helicopter, through the rugged beauty of the hills and canyons beyond the city limits.

After eluding the posse, including shooting down the helicopter and taking a more dangerous route through the canyons in order to keep his horse with him, the cowboy dies in a traffic accident. Trying to ride his horse across a busy highway at night, the horse panics, and they are both hit by a tractor-trailer driven by an ill, harried, over-tired teamster. (*The Brave Cowboy* was written in 1955, set in the immediate past when Harry Truman is the president on the wall behind the sheriff. The conflict centres on the refusal of a friend of the cowboy's to register for the draft. The cowboy, a veteran, is eventually wanted on a similar charge because he will not bother to carry any identification of any sort at all.)

In the other works in which they are used, symbolic environmental contrasts appear in a variety of ways, with differing degrees of emphasis. In *If*, for example, Mick and a friend steal a motorcycle, pick up a girl, then drive majestically through silent country lanes and green English fields. In *Cuckoo's Nest*, McMurphy promotes a sea-fishing trip. Out beyond the sight of land, in the elemental atmosphere of open sea and sky, the asylum patients lose much of their odd behaviour and hospital-induced symptoms, rediscover lost skills and pleasures, catch record-breaking fish while McMurphy stays in the cabin of the boat with a prostitute. In *They Shoot Horses, Don't They?* nature is reduced to glimpses of sunsets through a half-open back door, and the lapping of waves upon the pilings of the pier upon which the marathon dance hall is located.

In the film *Walkabout*, on the other hand, the concept of sterile imprisonment is conveyed by only a few shots of the city and of some apartment buildings. Otherwise, almost all the film is concerned with vividly evoking the sublime, savage, natural beauty and natural vitality and virtue of the Australian desert, a wild paradise, the film makes clear, on the brink of extinction from the effects of the oncoming intrusions of white civilization. (Ironically, just before they make their final charge from the Bolivian cantina, Butch will suggest to Sundance that they try Australia next.)

The bikers of *Easy Rider* finance their trek through the stark beauty of the southwest by selling drugs to a wealthy pervert in a Rolls-Royce underneath a freeway overpass by an airport as a jetliner lands, screaming, overhead.

Both the Jail and the Field, it seems to me, come from long and respectable traditions in fiction and philosophy, traditions in which words such as Utopia, Lilliput, Rousseau, the noble savage, Wordsworth, Eden, Prometheus figure largely. At the moment, however, it is more interesting to me to note the repeated choice of the jail rather than the family, the military, the rich (or their mansions) or even the police as symbols for repression, and the fondness for not just wild, but basically barren and superficially hostile natural environments.

The particular choices here seem to me to indicate a number of things. First, of course, is the extreme polarity of the opposition. There is no room for compromise and accommodation between them. Second, is the particular indictment of society made through use of the jail. Jail is not a weapon of an oppressive aristocracy, nor of illegal or corrupt authority. On the contrary, it exists, in theory, as a function of the general will and assent of all members of the society equally, and if not the end of due process, it is, at least, the effective termination of a process sanctioned in law. Jail does not serve a minority, it expresses the constitutional will of all the people, represents Society's values in the widest possible terms. Third, is the rejection of the idea of a benevolent Nature. The countryside, or desert, apparently barren and hostile, stands for the totally natural condition in which man survives, almost in the face of nature, through his innate, native abilities —intelligence, cunning, skill, tenacity as an individual. In opposition to the social immersion of the jail, the desert emphasizes the ultimate individual.

BOOKS AND FILMS

Books

Abbey, Edward. *The Brave Cowboy.* New York: Dodd, Mead, 1956.

Fonda, Peter, et al. *Easy Rider.* New York: New American Library, 1969.

Goldman, William. *Butch Cassidy and the Sundance Kid.* New York: Bantam, 1969.

Heller, Joseph. *Catch-22.* New York: Simon and Schuster, 1961.

Herlihy, James Leo. *Midnight Cowboy.* New York: Simon and Schuster, 1965.

Kesey, Ken. *One Flew Over the Cuckoo's Nest.* New York: Viking, 1962.

Marshall, James Vance. *The Children [Walkabout].* London: Michael Joseph, 1959.

McCoy, Horace. *They Shoot Horses, Don't They?* New York: Harold Matson, 1935. (with screenplay by Robert E. Thompson. New York: Avon, 1969.)

Sanders, Lawrence. *The Anderson Tapes.* New York: Putnam's, 1969.

Sherwin, David. *If . . . . .* London: Sphere, 1969.

Solzhenitsyn, Aleksandr I. *The First Circle,* trans. Thomas P. Whitney. New York: Harper and Row, 1968.

Films

The Anderson Tapes. Columbia, 1971.

Bonnie and Clyde. Warner Bros., 1967.

Butch Cassidy and the Sundance Kid.   Twentieth Century-Fox, 1969.

Catch-22. Paramount, 1970.

Easy Rider. Columbia, 1969.

If . . . . . Paramount, 1969.

Midnight Cowboy. United Artists, 1969.

Scandalous John. Walt Disney, 1971.

They Shoot Horses, Don't They? ABC Pictures, 1969.

Walkabout. Raab/Litvinoff, 1969.

THE CASE OF THE SPURIOUS SPINSTER

By PATRICIA KANE
Perry Mason: Modern Culture Hero

Perry Mason, a man of reason who wins his battles by his wit
without recourse to violence, is a modern culture hero. He is in a
long line of intellectual heroes, as distinguished from the physical
hero, which goes back through, among many others, Brer Rabbit,
Coyote, Sherlock Holmes, Auguste Dupin, at least to Ulysses, "the
wily one." Mason, who is as prodigious as other ratiocinative super-
men, is a clear-cut example of the popular hero—one who was created
by a known author and disseminated through the popular media.

Perry Mason is the creation of Erle Stanley Gardner, a lawyer-
turned-novelist, whose sheer output in printed books sounds like a
tall tale. Since his first Perry Mason novel in 1933 (*The Case of the
Velvet Claws*), Gardner has averaged three or four books a year, with
a total of over one hundred. As might be expected in the work of
so prolific a writer, the Perry Mason novels follow a pattern.

The formula has proved to be a popular one. Gardner's books
often sell in excess of one million copies. Although, according to
Alice Hackett's study *Seventy Years of Best Sellers*, the highest selling
Perry Mason book—*The Case of the Lucky Legs*, first published in
1934—has been exceeded in sales by seven Mickey Spillane and two
Ian Fleming tales, of the 151 crime, suspense, and espionage novels
that have sold more than one million copies, ninety-one are by Erle

Stanley Gardner. The ninety-one are mostly Perry Mason stories, but also include some about "the D.A." and several detective novels written under the pen name A.A. Fair.[1]   Although Gardner's books usually are not included in conventional bestseller lists because the sales are cumulative, that is, not all in one year, and mostly in paperback, his popularity is undisputed. In any given year his sales from several novels sometimes exceed five million.[2]   The Perry Mason television series made Mason a familiar hero to even larger audiences. After ten successful years, the series has begun what probably will be a vigorous second life in re-runs.

Gardner's biographer argues that Perry Mason's popularity stems from the "average American's fondness for legal problems" and from the essential drama of murder trials.[3]   An equally compelling reason seems to be that the hero serves the readers some legal citations, Latin phrases, and courtroom fireworks with their detective fare. Accurate detail about esoteric legal processes combines with an unreal world in which the innocent are never punished because truth always wins. The world of Perry Mason is a world in which all the facts are available so that a reasoned conclusion is possible.

Perry Mason may be the most unbelievable as well as the best-known lawyer in recent American fiction. As a criminal lawyer, specializing in murder trials, if Mason is not Prince Charming, he is a dragon slayer, a Galahad whose flair for reasoning and access to all relevant data combine with his virtuous concern for his client to save the innocent and restore order. Mason is almost a caricature of a hero. His skill and virtue, as well as his luck in always having innocent clients, even though he may know nothing about them or their guilt when he begins a case, are superhuman. Mason's extraordinary qualities are underlined by the fact that other lawyer characters lack either Mason's gifts or his ethics. Mason's popularity may suggest something of what Americans imagine about lawyers or, at least, their willingness to accept a lawyer as a spectacular hero and champion of justice.

The formula varies little from novel to novel. When Mason's client is charged with murder, his story sounds unreal, evidence against him seems overwhelming, but he is innocent. Mason cautions his client to tell him the truth because his defense will rely on it. Mason's private detective, who has a large firm with apparently

limitless resources and contacts in most cities in the area, compiles
facts on which Mason's solution usually depends. Mason unravels
the mystery in a courtroom, frequently during a preliminary hearing.
The real criminal often has framed Mason's client. Before Mason's
last-minute resolution, based either on new evidence or something
brought out in cross-examination, Mason will have done something
unorthodox, though never illegal, to protect his client and perhaps
be threatened with a hearing before the grievance committee of the
Bar Association. Mason demonstrates his skill as a trial lawyer as
well as his gift for reasoning in each novel. He ends with the client's
innocence established, his own behavior vindicated, and usually
with a substantial fee.

The formula of the Mason novels leaves no doubt unresolved.
The guilty person almost always confesses in that imaginary world.
The murdered person is never anyone whose loss will impoverish
society. The police and district attorney are not evil men who
arrest and prosecute for the joy of conviction without regard for
guilt because always there is substantial evidence that points to
Mason's client. The state's case errs because of incomplete information. Mason himself does not have the facts necessary to establish
the guilt of another until his dramatic revelation during a hearing or
a trial. The client is young, attractive, worthy of all the zeal of
Mason. The innocent are winsome; the guilty and the dead are
usually unsavory.

Mason is a superhuman hero whose energies and talents serve
others. He was born into fiction at the full height of his powers. He
has no family, and his origins, education, and apprentice days in
practice remain unexplained. His fame and success depend entirely
on his skill, not on any advantage of birth. He follows the pattern
of many American heroes in that he operates alone. His secretary
and his private detective serve as confidants, but Mason has no
partners and never associates in a case with other lawyers on a basis
of equality. His secretary usually calls him "chief," an accurate
estimate of his position. Like traditional heroes, Mason performs
miraculous exploits. His feats are not achieved by magic, however,
but by intelligence, hard work, and knowledge of technology and
law. When he explains his reasoning, it can be understood by all,
including presumably a jury, although a jury never has to weigh

evidence and arguments in a Mason novel. Only one conclusion, Mason's, is possible, and all are agreed.

Mason gives his entire life to saving his clients. He has no family to distract him, no social life, no civic concerns. He can go without sleep and postpone meals. He apparently does other unspecified legal work; at least once in each novel his secretary nags him gently about urgent correspondence or briefs, but Mason is bored by such routine, and it can be postponed. His loyal secretary and his private detective also forego normal life in service of Mason and truth and justice. Sympathy stays with Mason despite the superior gifts that would seem to make it superfluous because the odds against him appear insurmountable. At least once, all believe that Mason will lose. When this nadir is reached, Mason redoubles his reasoning and the direction changes abruptly. It takes Mason's singular talents and hard work to allay the forces of unjust suspicion.

The Mason stories picture a potentially threatening world. Indeed without Mason to save them, scores of innocent persons would have been executed. Only Mason stands between them and unjust conviction. The threat never seems very real in the novels, however, because readers know that there will be a solution posed that provides a happy ending. Mason's clients are not just acquitted, the true story is known. No other innocent person will be charged with that crime.

Implicit in Gardner's books is faith in the adversary system as a means to establish truth. Such faith is not always shared by serious students of justice, some of whom argue that it is not the advocate's job to pursue abstract truth, but to act as partisan for his client and insist on procedural safeguards. Such a system requires that opposing counsel be equally matched, a requisite less true in life than in Mason novels.[4] The adversary system is well served in fiction, however, and provides excitement that the more usual non-trial work of lawyers would not. It is an admirable showcase for one of Mason's endowments.

Gardner has spelled out Mason's special virtues, which in his view are shared by most lawyers, who know that "they are the high priests and priestesses in the temple of justice; that their duty is to their clients, to the courts and to the public." Gardner remarks that Mason's dedication to his clients and to justice sometimes makes him take desperate chances, but that even those lawyers who question his methods "admire his loyalty and sheer fighting ability."[5] Mason's devotion to his client and to truth are the central ingredients in his professional life. No matter how bizzare the client's story, if Mason believes it is true, he looks for evidence to support it; whatever seems to contradict the client's story, he never wavers in his fight. He risks his professional reputation, and very occasionally his life, to serve his client and establish the truth.

Although Mason risks his reputation, he would never violate the law or defeat justice. He distinguishes between crimes and what he thinks of as his sharp tricks, and he will not violate the limits he sets for himself. Mason says that he never assumes that a client is guilty because that would mean substituting his judgment for that of a court, but if he knew a client was guilty, that would be different. What that difference would be is not made explicit because Mason never has a guilty client, but it is suggested by his remark that as an officer of the court he represents justice, that his function is not to use his brains to "try to stand between a guilty client and the law of the land."[6] Mason's feeling for his client is evoked (in *The Case of the Horrified Heirs,* 1964) in his observation that a lawyer suffers with his clients in a way that a doctor does not suffer with his patients because a lawyer always can help his client. In a world where a lawyer can make things better, many means short of law-breaking are permitted.

Mason's clients are served by extraordinary expertise. Mason's knowledge of criminal practice is formidable, but believable in a specialist. His knowing the latest rules about search warrants and the right of accused to counsel seems authentic. Similarly, his familiarity with forensic medicine and his easy mastery of the essentials about fingerprints, ballistics, poison, and even weather conditions are not impossible for a specialist. Credulity is strained, however, when Mason's information seemingly extends to all fields of law and rarely requires checking. His total recall can be unintentionally funny, including as it frequently does full citation of cases. One instance of Mason's mastery of bibliography that borders on the ludicrous occurs in *The Case of the Grinning Gorilla,* 1952. When he encounters unexpected evidence during a trial, Mason tries to get a recess so that he can consult again a scientific treatise about the similarity of the blood of gorillas and humans. When the request is denied, Mason, who apparently never uses notes in court, remembers enough to get an expert witness to request time to study this article in his field. In addition to knowing the conclusions and something of the methodology of the research, Mason remembers the title of the journal the findings appear in, the date, the volume, and the page numbers. One wonders what prodigious wonders might have transpired if Mason had been able to refresh his memory.

Mason's extraordinary knowledge and respect for facts, the traditional province of a jury, suggests that Gardner's novels might emphasize the jury system. Such is not the case, however, although the jury system is never criticized. Juries are simply superfluous when one of Mason's gifts addresses himself to a problem. Often Mason solves the case at a preliminary hearing at which no jury is present. When there is a trial, the jury is vague and scarcely a felt presence. Mason apparently spends little time and effort in choosing a jury. Despite his extensive use of private detectives in investigating the persons connected with the crime, he does not investigate the jurors or know them as individuals. No space is given in the novels to the process of jury selection; the narrative at most includes Mason's statement that the jury is satisfactory. The jury does not deliberate in the usual sense. The decision is very clear, either because a witness confesses while testifying or because Mason presents proof to the judge in chambers. The district attorney may move to dismiss, or the judge may direct a verdict. The jury is not asked to weigh conflicting evidence and reach a just verdict. Essentially Mason's arguments are directed to the judge, another expert. Unlike the jury, the judge is not vague. He is a character who is named and who plays an active part in the trial scenes. He is always a judge who cares about the truth and the rights of the accused. There are no wicked or poorly trained judges either in trial courts or in the lower courts that conduct preliminary hearings. Apparently none commits a reversible error, although that is only a surmise because only the defendant has a right to appeal, and the defendant is never convicted. Mason's courtroom fireworks are not so much a show for the jury as they are directed toward a solution of the mystery.

Perry Mason, hero, differs not just from other lawyers in Gardner's novels, but also from lawyers in serious American fiction. Mason's combined talents as detective and courtroom advocate bear some superficial resemblance to Mark Twain's Pudd'n-head Wilson in that both untangle mistaken identities and produce courtroom surprises, but Mason never experiences public rejection like Wilson's. On the contrary, he enjoys widespread fame and acceptance, which aid him in his work. Faulkner's Gavin Stevens (in *Knight's Gambit* and the Snopes novels) also can be both detective and advocate, uses unorthodox methods to discover truth, and displays more intelligence than most. Stevens, however, is capable of error, has clients who may be poor or guilty or both, and inhabits a society in which reason does not prevail so easily. Faulkner's Horace Benbow (in *Sanctuary*) is another skilled detective, but he must try his case in a hostile atmosphere before an incompetent judge. Whereas Mason always exposes witnesses who lie, Benbow has no opportunity to reveal perjury. Mason resembles not at all the cynical defense lawyers of Dreiser's *An American Tragedy*. He would not have a guilty client nor invent a story for him to tell. Mason's world is one of clear issues with no such ambiguities about responsibility and guilt as those in Dreiser's novel. Mason encounters no hard necessity which requires him to compromise as do Cozzens's lawyers, nor develop the wry detachment of Auchincloss's Wall Street lawyers. In short, Mason is the lawyer character of popular culture, not of serious fiction.

Nor does Mason bear much resemblance to most modern criminal lawyers. Mason's fame and position are unquestioned, but the criminal lawyer generally has lower status in the community and the bar than a civil lawyer. Mason's clients are respectable persons of at least middle-class station. The more usual pattern in criminal practice involves lower-class clients, since ninety percent of the arrests and convictions for crime are in the lower class. Mason is in solo practice as are the majority of lawyers, but those in solo practice are the lowest paid members of the profession, whereas Mason earns large fees and has funds of his own to expend in behalf of a client. If Mason has any resemblance to reality, it would be to the small number of lawyers of national reputation who defend upper-class clients in criminal cases. His record of acquittals, how-ever, is certainly unmatched by even the most able criminal lawyers.[7]

What inferences can one draw from the Perry Mason novels

that so little resemble life? Most obviously, one can observe the
conventions of popular fiction, especially the detective story in
which a man of reason triumphs in a rational world. Perry Mason is
as much a detective as he is a lawyer and resembles the detective
hero invented by Edgar Allan Poe and developed by Conan Doyle.
Gardner's detective hero in the A.A. Fair books differs little from
Mason as detective. The courtroom ingredient in the Mason books
is important, however. It is a dramatic device whereby Mason con-
fronts the forces of government represented by the district attorney.

The fact that Mason has proved so much more popular than Gardner's
district attorney hero suggests that readers locate the enemy less in
individual criminals than in government, that freeing the innocent
is more interesting than convicting the guilty. Mason may reflect a
comfortable version of anarchy in his opposition to government.
Although Mason never violates the law, he skirts the edge and treats
the police as honorable but mistaken enemies whom he does not
trust until he has all the facts. Mason's insistence that his clients
refuse to talk to the police reflects a contempt for their ability to
use information more than it does a concern for due process. Since
the police and the district attorney are so capable of error, constitutional safeguards are essential to protect the innocent. Mason
never displays concern for the rights of the guilty who blurt out
confessions in court under his restless probing, however. Since
Mason is right and his motives pure, he is admired for actions that
in the police are wrong. Neither Mason nor the police resort to
physical force, but both try to get confessions from persons who
have not consulted counsel. Whether those admissions can be used
in a subsequent trial is not part of Mason's concern or Gardner's
fiction. Mason violates no law and, as is seemly in an advocate, is
loyal to his client against all others.

Perry Mason, as a proper hero, champions right and wins. Like
heroes he also represents a nostalgic longing for a simpler time. In an
age when the courtroom advocacy is no longer the norm for lawyers, in
which lawyers are specialists who can rarely be understood when they
speak in their specialties except by other lawyers, Mason appears in
court and speaks so that all can understand. It is true that the rules
of evidence remain occult information of which Mason is a master,
but the important facts that establish guilt and innocence are clear.
Mason works without partners in an age when few successful lawyers

do. He reflects a nostalgia for the man-of-reason advocate who devotes himself to persons not corporations or government. Mason is up to date in his information, but old-fashioned in his appeal. Like other heroes he uses his superhuman abilities to make the world pleasanter for the ordinary persons who depend on him. He restores a rational order by seeking and finding truth in a world suitable for a hero, a world without uncertainty, ambiguity, or—thanks to Perry Mason—injustice.

NOTES

[1] Alice Payne Hackett, *Seventy Years of Best Sellers*: 1895-1965 (New York, R.R. Bowker, 1967), pp. 64-70.

[2] James D. Hart, *The Popular Book: A History of America's Literary Taste* (New York: Oxford University Press, 1950), pp. 259-60.

[3] Alva Johnston, *The Case of Erle Stanley Gardner* (New York: William Morrow and Company, 1947), p. 15.

[4] For an attack on the adversary system as a means to truth, see Jerome Frank, *Courts on Trial: Myth and Reality in American Justice* (Princeton: Princeton University Press, 1950). The weakness of the system is that the outcome may depend on the skill of the opposing lawyers rather than truth or justice; Robert Traver, *Small Town D.A.* (New York: E.P. Dutton and Company, 1954), pp. 210-212. (Traver is the pen name of John Voelker, Michigan lawyer, district attorney, and judge.) Whatever the merits of the adversary system, Americans think of law as a trial in court; Willard Hurst, "Changing Popular Views About Law," *Anals of American Academy*, CCLXXXVI (May 1953), 1.

[5] *Waylaid Wolf*, pp. v-vi.

[6] *Glamorous Ghost*, p. 129.

[7] The facts about criminal practice are from C. Ray Jeffery, "The Legal Profession," *Society and the Law: New Meanings for an Old Profession*, F. James Davis, Henry H. Foster, Jr., C. Ray Jeffery, and E. Eugene Davis (New York: The Free Press of Glencoe, 1962), pp. 328, 329, 336. Mason's success exceeds that of any well-known twentieth-century trial lawyer. For accounts of the cases of some of them, see Gene Fowler, *The Great Mouthpiece: A Life Story of William J. Fallon* (New York: Crown, 1931); Clarence Darrow, *Attorney for the Damned*, ed. Arthur Weinberg (New York: Simon and Schuster, 1957); John Wesley Noble and Bernard Averbuch, *Never Plead Guilty: The Story of Jake Ehrlich* (New York: Farrar, Straus and Cudahy, 1955); Melvin M. Belli, *Ready for the Plaintiff!: A Story of Personal Injury Law* (New York: Henry Holt and Company, 1956).

By MARSHALL McLUHAN
The Popular Hero and Anti-Hero

In *True Grit,* John Wayne plays a parody of himself. He turns the traditional Western hero into an anti-hero. All the resourcefulness and daring of the frontiersman are poured out on the cowboy's coffin, as it were—a whole crock of red-eye, but it has first been processed through his kidneys.

The savvy of the great frontiersman has been purchased for twenty-five bucks by a young New England girl who seeks to avenge her father's murder. She buys the individual skill and daring of the frontiersman, making sure to have him sign legal documents at every turn. She is the New England matriarch, skilled in all corporate defences of legalism. In short, *True Grit* is a capsule summary of both the Western hero as entrepreneur and the eastern lawyer as the creator of corporate safety.

It is characteristic of all social processes that they become manifest and conspicuous at the moment of their demise.

Patterns only emerge at moments of intense stress, and such stress is the result of overload. Such is the world of medical symptomology, for example. The medical man is trained to recognize only acute symptoms, just as he is trained to treat such symptoms rather than their causes. (The Chinese doctors are paid not to cure but to keep their

135

patients well.) In his book *The Stress of Life,* Hans Selye demonstrates that all illness is the effort of the body to restrain the spread of invading organisms. This applies, naturally, to "sick" jokes as much as to sick people or societies. "He has a fine head of skin."

The WASP can't see culture as fun, nor can he see "pop kulch" as serious: "Life is short; our faces must be long." His plight reminds us of Tarzan's last desperate cry: "Who greased my vine?"

True Grit, by manifesting stark symptoms of the extreme form of individual enterprise and the extreme forms of corporate legal safety, calls attention to massive changes in these areas. The conglomerate as a form of hijacking in current business development expresses the end of the corporation as a safety mechanism, as much as *True Grit* underscores the end of heroic individualism.

The anti-hero became a theme in art and literature as early as Thackeray's *Vanity Fair,* the "novel without a hero." Characteristically, the "hero" of the book is Becky Sharp, the "mother" of Scarlet O'Hara. The heroism of New England's Pilgrim Fathers has gone through the vanishing point.

Marshall Fishwick, in *The Hero, American Style,* points out that the phrase "self-made man" was first used by Henry Clay in an 1832 Congressional debate. There is no better example of the fateful contraries that lurk in any intensely stressed form than the case of Henry Ford. Just as much as John Wayne in *True Grit,* he became the parody of the self-made man simply by pushing it to the extreme. Fishwick points this out:

> Many turned the Alger words into flesh, but none with
> more lasting impact than Henry Ford. He stands at the spot
> where the farm and the factory meet. People who have never
> heard of Washington, Boone, or Bunyan know the name Ford
> well. It bounces over the world's highways daily. Under his
> guidance, the automobile became for us what the cross had
> been for the Emperor Constantine: *In hoc signo vinces.*

The Ford car, by speeding up the old horse and buggy and by putting everybody on the open road to pursue distant goals and dreams, destroyed both the open road and the goal and dream. It all came to rest in Greenfield Village, as much a cemetery of forgotten values as any garden city.

****

The Associated Press reported from Washington, D.C. on July 20, 1970:

> A presidential commission recommended yesterday a
> radical reorganization of the Defense Department—including
> the removal of the Joint Chiefs of Staff from involvement
> in military operation—and a number of other steps designed
> to achieve more efficiency and save money in weapons pro-
> curement.

Such leaders, whether military or civilian, are merely *matching* the errors of the past rather than *making* the history of the present. Consultants and executives alike are made into nineteenth-century men by their nineteenth-century production-line thinking. By trying to control the twentieth century with such means, they are elaborately qualified to make use of the nearest egress. Military leadership today is sitting in the ejection seat.

By JEROME RODNITZKY

A Pacifist St. Joan — The Odyssey of Joan Baez

The 1960's were particularly hard on American heroes. Even John Kennedy, a legendary martyr in 1963, had his memory badly tarnished by the ugly results of his foreign policy. Thus it is noteworthy that Joan Baez's intellectual image soared during a period of general cynicism. Her rise in esteem was mostly a matter of timing, for Joan rather grew up with the decade. In 1960, during the earliest days of Camelot, she was a largely unknown nineteen-year-old singer with a gifted voice and a penchant for Anglo-American folk ballads. As events grew darker in 1963 and after, she gradually became an activist, both in the area of civil rights and universal nonviolence. In 1964 she demonstrated her concern symbolically, by refusing to pay that portion of her income tax (60%) designated for defense spending.[1] The following year she funded an Institute For the Study of Nonviolence, headquartered in her hometown—Carmel, California.[2]

Baez's early diatribes against the nation-state were usually vague, but the accelerating Vietnam War documented most of her points. Joan was frankly and consistently radical in an age of polarization, and pacifist in an era of increasing violence. More importantly, she addressed herself to the problems of universal man, at a time when many American youths were vomiting on nationalism. Above all, there was her singing, which compensated for her early intellectual

139

shallowness and general inarticulateness. Throughout the 1960's her crystal-clear voice soared through the soprano register, high above the political and social struggles. Always the most artful, distinct singer in the folk field, Joan shifted her repertory from the ancient balladry, to protest songs, to Bob Dylan's prose songs, to country-and-western, and finally to her own compositions. Baez's record albums always sold well, but were never best sellers; and this relative lack of commercial popularity protected her political credibility. As the child of a decade of agitation, her attitudes and lifestyle evolved so smoothly that she seemed not to have changed at all. Joan blended into the protest tradition, into pacifism, into activism, into a publicized marriage and motherhood, into a vicarious martyr-dom (as her husband, David Harris, went to jail for draft resistance), and finally into a national symbol for nonviolence.

Baez was an unlikely cultural hero. Born in Staten Island, New York, in 1941, she was one of three sisters. Her father, a Mexican-born physicist, and her mother, of Scotch-English ancestry, met at Drew University in Madison, New Jersey, and the family moved around the country while Dr. Baez pursued his career as a researcher and consultant. The family's strong religious background may explain Joan's moral fervor. Her maternal grandfather was an Episcopal minister, while her paternal grandfather was a Catholic turned Metho-dist clergyman. Moreover, her parents were converted to the Quaker faith, though Joan remains religiously nonaligned. After attending high school in Palo Alto, California, she moved to Boston with her family in 1959 and became a college dropout after a month at Boston University. By this time her completely untrained voice was already striking enough to make her a local star at Boston Coffeehouses. The folk boom was just beginning (especially around the Eastern colleges) and Baez picked up songs and guitar technique from a number of semi-professional folksingers. That Summer, Joan was a surprise sensation at the Newport Folk Festival, and she soon signed a re-cording contract with Vanguard Records—a small company which retained her loyalty for twelve years. Baez's initial record was re-leased in 1960, followed by the first of many successful college-oriented concert tours, and Joan Baez was suddenly America's premier folksinger. She was all of twenty years of age.[3]

Like Bob Dylan, another famous folk dropout, Joan rejected a college education. Indeed, in 1967, she asserted that college was

another way for parents "to hang on to their children." She could
see putting up with the "trivia of college" to get professional training, but not because "your parents or society says you should."[4]
Joan felt she "rebelled so completely" against education because
her father's academic standing obligated her to be a "student-type."
Dr. Baez had often disapproved of her ideas on "nonviolence and
anti-nationalism;" and she noted with obvious satisfaction that though
he "was peace-marching long before" his daughter, her radical swing
left him "looking and acting . . . fairly moderate."[5] Thus, moving
to her father's left in regard to education and pacifism might have
been part of a personal rebellion. In any case, Joan received a unique
social education. American society was teaching a variety of lessons
and she learned fast. Baez was immediately attracted to the civil
rights crusade, probably because of her own childhood exposure to
racism. Joan grew up in Redlands, California in a cultural limbo.
Her father had professional status, but she was not accepted by
whites because she was dark and part Mexican, while the Mexican
population disowned her because she could not speak Spanish. Later,
when the family moved to Clarence Center, New York, a town of
800 people, Joan felt that "as far as they knew we were niggers."[6]

Baez was one of many folksingers who actively supported civil
rights. For example, when she attended the rally that climaxed the
"March on Washington" in August 1963, Bob Dylan, Peter-Paul-&-
Mary, and others performed with her. Yet, none of these had risked
personal harm as Joan had, when she escorted a little black girl to her
integrated school through a hostile crowd in Birmingham, Alabama
earlier that year. Nor did protest singers tend to physically involve
themselves in activities such as the Student Free Speech Movement
and the early protests against the Vietnam War. Joan was often a
physical activist. For example, in December 1964, at the University
of California's Berkeley campus, Baez helped draw a large crowd to
a rally protesting the banning of certain campus political activities
and then marched into the University's administration building at
the head of 1,000 undergraduates who occupied the building for
fifteen hours.[7]

On June 8, 1965, Joan sang at the SANE Emergency Rally on
Vietnam, in Madison Square Garden, but before performing she told
the crowd:

This is mainly to the young people here, but really to every-

> body. . . . You must listen to your heart and do what it dic-
> tates . . . If you feel that to . . . go to war is wrong, you have
> to say no to the draft. And if you young ladies think it is
> wrong to kill . . . you can say yes to the young men who say
> no to the draft.[8]

In August, 1965, Joan joined 1,000 anti-Vietnam demonstrators in picketing the White House. She later commented: "I don't think the President gives a damn."[9] Although it would be almost three years before she met her husband, David Harris, marriage to a draft resistor seemed almost inevitable. And thus in 1966, there appeared a poster which pictured the three Baez sisters on a bench, staring straight ahead, with the caption: "Girls Say Yes to Boys Who Say No."

After continuing her anti-War and civil rights activities in 1966, Baez made her first concert tour abroad when she visited Japan in January, 1967. However, at her Tokyo concert, which was later shown on Japanese television, the Japanese translator admitted that he omitted all of Baez's political remarks at the urging of a man who identified himself as a CIA agent. Thus, when Joan explained the song, "What Have They Done to the Rain" (about atomic fallout), the translator stated only that "the show was being televised." When she interpreted her subtle anti-war song, "Saigon Bride," he said only: "This is a song about the Vietnam War." And when Joan told the audience she had refused to pay her taxes as a protest against the Vietnam War, the translator said only: "Taxes are high in the United States." On balance, Joan's trip was not a political success. She said she came to Japan "first as a human being, second as a pacifist, and third as a folksinger." However, the Japanese tended to accept her primarily as a folksinger, only secondarily as a human being, and hardly at all as a pacifist.[10]

Back in the United States, Joan became more vigorous. She was arrested in Oakland, California in October, 1967 for blocking the Armed Forces Induction Center and served a ten-day prison sentence. Two months later she served a month for the same offense. Her mother, then fifty-four years old, accompanied her both times, or as Joan put it: "My Mother's been to jail with me twice now. We did civil disobedience together."[11] During her October sit-in, Joan met David Harris for the first time. In a rather unique courtship, Harris visited Joan during her second jail term, and they agreed to tour colleges and selected cities to speak for draft resistance. Joan would usually give a concert, and then David and she would speak about the resistance. In the middle of their tour, in March, 1968, they were married. On May 29, 1968, Harris, then twenty-two years old and a former Stanford University student body president, was sentenced to three years in prison for refusing induction into the Armed Forces. To avoid media coverage, the government finally took him into custody July 16, 1969—the day the Apollo 11 moon-shot started. In December, 1969 Joan gave birth to their son, Gabriel, and after a few months continued to travel around the country singing and espousing her nonviolent philosophy while her husband served his sentence.[12]

The shock of David's incarceration seemed to produce a new Joan Baez. Most people noticed that she cut her long hair (once a distinct trademark), but her mental change was far more striking. The uncertain, often petulant folksinger, suddenly became a confident, aggressive extemporaneous speaker. Her appearance on national television talk shows was a good example. As a guest on the now defunct "Alan Burke Show" in 1967, Baez had been browbeaten and put on the defensive by the generally shallow Burke. The following year, when she and David appeared on "The Les Crane Show," Joan had sung songs, but let David do most of the talking. However, a year later, on "The Dick Cavett Show," a month after David's imprisonment, she completely confounded Cavett's attempt at witty superficiality with a moving and articulate explanation of her pacifist philosophy. Joan so outpointed the usually glib, if not profound, Cavett that the next day Howard K. Smith was moved to use the commentary portion of his nightly news show to respond to Baez's arguments. Smith called Joan "one of our high income revolutionaries," and dismissed her as an idealist who naively believed that revolution would bring perfection out of ruins. Smith contended that America was a middle-class country which abhorred revolution and that the path to progress was one of slow "precinct work" in elections and legislation.[13]

There was also a noticeable change in Baez's concert appearances. She insisted that tickets to her performances could cost no more than two dollars, and she developed a more commanding stage presence. In September, 1970, for example, she demonstrated her new confidence at a concert in Sopot, Poland. After singing "Blowin in the

Wind," and a Beatle song, she explained why David was in prison
(through a translator) and then sang one of her own compositions,
which she dedicated to the young Poles who she felt were in the
same position as American youths—"hitchhiking but with no place
to go." Afterward at a press conference, when asked about America's
"sickness," she replied: "America is not the sickest but the biggest.
If Poland was as big as America, she might be just as destructive."
The translator omitted the last part of her answer.[14] Back home she
was now considered more dangerous. On February 3, 1971 Miami,
Florida officials refused to allow her to give a college-sponsored
concert in the city's Marine Stadium, arguing that her appearance
might present a "problem of crowd control."[15] Yet she was never
a direct political threat. People were generally unwilling to hear her
speak unless she also sang. During her February, 1971 tour she drew
7,000 people to a paid concert, but only 400 showed up for a free
political talk.[16]

David Harris was paroled, March 15, 1971, after serving twenty
months of his three-year sentence. Meanwhile, Joan had been in
good form on talk shows. Upon her return to "The Dick Cavett
Show," the somewhat chastened host introduced her as "the leading
lady of American folk music." Despite this respectful introduction,
Baez's manner was very condescending. She obviously resented
Dick's mild attempts at levity and treated him as a somewhat backward child. The conversation centered on prisons and Joan observed
that incarceration was educative. Since bank robbers came out of
prison better bank robbers, she argued: "If you go into prison a
pacifist, you come out a better pacifist." Cavett later noted that
prisons were bad, but asked Joan what society should do with
serious criminals, like murderers. She replied: "If you talk about
serious murderers, they are not in our jails, they are running nations."
A month later Baez faced a generally hostile audience on the "David
Frost Show" although Frost himself was sympathetic. Here she
adopted a lecture stance and noted that though people were afraid
of chaos if they did not have government, our government was
chaotic. She argued that Americans were "disciplined to the point
where" they could not even think, and thus were insulated from
"the Cambodian Mother whose child has been burned." Joan's
solution was to work outside the system to build a society that did
not "corrupt people." She felt it was impossible to reform the system

itself and when asked to sing a song that reflected her present mood, she sang, "Heaven Help Us All."[17] Critics could point out that Baez still came up with simplistic, one-dimensional answers, but there was a new strangely effective power in her verbal arguments. The often shy folksinger had suddenly become a rather charismatic agitator. Looking back, it is ironic that Bob Dylan, now perhaps the most reclusive of the pop singers, criticized Baez for her passiveness and lack of revelance. In 1962 Dylan observed:

> It ain't nothin' just to walk around and sing . . . you have to step out a little, right? Take Joanie man, she's still singing about Mary Hamilton. I mean where's that at? She's walked around on picket lines, she's got all kinds of feeling, so why ain't she steppin' out?[18]

Although by 1965 Dylan completely rejected activism or even relevance and had literally dropped out physically, Joan did indeed step out. Other serious and gifted folksingers like Judy Collins sang Malvina Reynold's song, "It Isn't Nice," about how it wasn't nice "to block the doorways" and "go to jail." However, Baez actually sat in the doorways and went to jail. While other former topical singers turned to catchy top-ten ballads and cashed in on television guest appearances, Joan put out an average of one record per year, sang college-circuit concerts, and invested most of her money in causes like her own Institute. In an era when credibility became the magic word, it is not hard to understand why Joan Baez's star was in the ascendancy.

Joan's personal philosophy of non-violence has become increasingly sophisticated. Her two major influences have been Ira Sandperl, a veteran of West Coast pacifist crusades, and David Harris, her husband. In 1964, Joan asked Sandperl to tutor her on the philosophy of non-violence and the lessons turned into The Institute for the Study of Nonviolence. Sandperl, now 48 years old, has remained the guiding influence behind the Institute. Founded in 1965, the School is just beginning to focus its energy on specific goals. Brief workshops and pacifist philosophy remain the heart of the Institute's program. However, the communal living, an integral part of the workshops, is now being applied locally through experiments with land and food cooperatives and political action groups.[19] David Harris's influence on Baez has largely been one of emphasis. His philosophy (set forth in his recent book, *Goliath*) is hazy, but he styles himself an organizer rather than a preacher, and Joan's new aggressiveness can be traced to her husband's vigorous brand of organized pacifism.[20] Joan probably summed up her present outlook in the following passage from *Daybreak*:

> The problem isn't Communism. The problem is consensus. There's a consensus out that it's OK to kill when your government decides who to kill. If you kill inside the country you get in trouble. If you kill outside the country, right time, right season, latest enemy, you get a medal. There are about 130 nation-states, and each of them thinks it's a swell idea to bump off all the rest because he is more important. The pacifist thinks there is only one tribe. Three billion members. They come first. We think killing any member of the family is a dumb idea. We think there are more decent and intelligent ways of settling differences. And man had better start investigating these other possibilities because if he doesn't, then by mistake or by design, he will probably kill off the whole damn race.[21]

At various times, Baez has stressed that music alone was not enough for her. In 1970 she observed that if she did not stand up for life in deed as well as in song, all those beautiful sounds were "irrelevant to the only real question of this century: How do we stop men from murdering each other."[22] Nevertheless, for millions of Americans she is her music. Divorced from her songs, she is incomplete. For Joan personally, the music is both hope and catharsis. "To sing," Joan wrote, "is to love and to affirm, to fly and soar, to coast into the hearts of the people who listen, to tell them that life is to live, that love is there, that nothing is a promise, but that beauty exists, and must be hunted for and found."[23] Yet, if her songs do give her wings, it is not apparent at her concerts. Baez's singing has a solemnity which is independent of her material and quickly transferred to the audience. People do not sway to her music, and hand-clapping would seem ludicrous. The fragile nature of her lyrics encourages people to protect them with a hushed silence. Her recent concerts are considerably looser because of the larger, less intimate audiences and her new outgoing style. The earlier concerts were rather mystical. I first heard Baez perform in November, 1962, at the University of Illinois. Dressed in a plain skirt and blouse, she walked onto the stage of an auditorium filled with 1500 students, sat down on a stool, and without a word started playing. After some forty minutes of songs, punctuated only by brief introductions and

the dedication of one song to Pete Seeger, she walked off at inter-
mission without any indication she was returning. The second half
of her program was a copy of the first. She ended her concert with
one encore and a simple, "thank you, goodnight." Yet, few faulted
her lack of showmanship. Baez's voice seemed completely independent
of the frail figure on the stage. At one point she quietly commanded
the audience: "Sing this one with me;" and the assembly sang along
in whispered voices as if they were in church. It is easy to understand
her magnetic effect at Woodstock in August, 1969, when at 2 a.m.
she stood, noticeably pregnant, singing to a dreamy sea of flower
children.

On her recordings, Baez's voice has recently lost some of its
magic, being rather overpowered by electronic sidemen and subverted
by echo chambers and sound-on-sound arrangements. Yet periodically,
as the accompaniment fades, her voice breaks through—all the stronger
in contrast. Balance has been the strong point of Joan's albums. She
never sang one type of song; and thus even her hard-core protest songs
were seldom tedious. Nevertheless, Joan always had critics. In regard
to her early albums, *Little Sandy Review,* headquarters for "folkier
than thou" criticism, conceded that Baez was "perhaps the most
thrilling young voice of our time," but sadly concluded that her vocal
gifts were "too rich and too grandiose to carry the simplicity of the
humble folk song." When the traditional singer like Woody Guthrie
or Leadbelly sang a folksong, the LSR reviewers argued, it described
"the basic nature of his land and people." Baez, however, could
only describe herself, for in "molding a song to her own powerful
personality" she destroyed it. Joan did not lack defenders. After
reviewing Baez's first album, the LSR reviewers noted that her many
fervent fans had requested that they "quit picking on Joan" and "go
back to beating" their "grandmothers with old Library of Congress
albums."[24] Likewise, Baez's 1969 dual album of Bob Dylan songs,
Any Day Now, was panned by Dylanologist Alan Weberman, because
"Joanie's sweet soprano voice" could not express the heavy contempt-
uous sarcasm of many of Dylan's songs.[25]

Yet Baez's albums, like Dylan's, resist generalizations. Unlike
Dylan's they show steady growth. Joan's first three albums contained
largely traditional folksongs, with the exception of Malvina Reynold's
low-key protest song, "What Have They Done to the Rain." In 1962
her fourth album reflected Dylan's influence. She sang two of his songs,

including a long pacifist ballad, "With God On Our Side." Her civil rights concern was represented by the "Battle Hymn of the Republic" and an audience participation rendition of "We Shall Overcome." Every song on the third and fourth albums was taped in concert. Her fifth album, in 1963, was a very mixed bag indeed. Along with one of Dylan's personal laments, "It Ain't Me Babe," there were Phil Och's social environmental ballad, "There But For Fortune," a Johnny Cash song, the usual traditional songs, and "Birmingham Sunday," Richard Farina's memorial to black children killed in a church bombing. Her next offering, in 1965, was much the same with a little more emphasis on Dylan—four of Bob's songs appeared including the title song, "Farewell Angelina," and his older warning of nuclear war, "A Hard Rain's A-Gonna Fall." After deciding not to release an album of rock-type songs in 1966, she replaced it with a Christmas album.[26] Joan supposedly vetoed the rock music because she had read that Gandhi "rejected art if it didn't represent truth— if it didn't elevate the soul." Rock-'n-roll was fun, but it failed to meet Gandhi's standards. "I still like to sing it sometimes," she said, "but it doesn't represent what I feel."[27]

As usual her 1967 album gave mixed indications of her real feelings. Titled *Joan*, the record had full orchestra accompaniment, and contained two songs Baez co-authored, "North" and "Saigon Bride"—the latter a rather profound anti-War ballad. *Baptism,* her next album, was a real change of pace and commercially her least successful venture. It featured a wide assortment of poems, both spoken and sung, centering on the sanctity of life. In 1969 there followed her dual-record set of Dylan songs and a homey album, dedicated to her imprisoned husband. The latter two records were made in Nashville and followed Bob Dylan's move toward a country- and-western emphasis. Like Dylan, Baez has continued to use many of the excellent Nashville-based sidemen for accompaniment. *One Day at a Time,* her 1970 entry, included her first individual composi- tions, "Sweet Sir Galahad" and "A Song For David"—both intensely personal and remarkably melodic ballads. The same year Vanguard released a two-record anthology of Joan's last ten years of songs. In 1971 Joan Baez reached maturity as a writer-performer with her dual- record album, *Blessed Are.* Baez wrote nine of its twenty songs, and taken as a whole they indicated her considerable promise as a writer. Joan's ballads, like her prose in *Daybreak*, are very uneven, but show flashes of brillance both in melody and lyrics. Presently, her style and melodies are usually ahead of her lyrics. *Blessed Are,* contains very diverse songs; yet, whereas the diversity of earlier records stemmed from her eclectic approach to music, the latest mix seems to be purposeful. Joan has steadily become more tolerant, and increasingly her songs have reflected the common conditions of all men. On *Blessed Are* she sings sympathetically about a Confederate soldier in Robbie Robertson's "The Night They Drove Old Dixie Down," about a "red-neck Georgia farmboy" in Mickey Newbury's "San Francisco Mabel Joy," and about middle-class Southern landholders in her own "Outside the Nashville City Limits." Add to these her renditions of Kris Kristofferson's "Help Me Make It Through the Night," Lennon-McCartney's "Let It Be," Ron Miller's "Heaven Help Us All," and her own title song, "Blessed Are," and you have a package that pointedly stresses universal togetherness. It appears that Baez's art and politics are finally coming together. The best indication of this is her latest album, *Come From the Shadows.* On the cover is a photo of an elderly couple involved in a protest demonstration— holding hands with one hand and showing the peace sign with the other—while two helmeted policemen stand by. On the back-cover Baez asks citizens "to take some risks. Stop paying war taxes, refuse the armed forces . . . give up the national state, share your money . . . in short, sisters and brothers, arm up with love and come from the shadows."

Of the album's twelve songs, Baez wrote six. Her songs included "Prison Trilogy," a protest against our prisons which ends by asking help to "raze the prisons to the ground," and "Bangladesh," a ballad describing the slaughter of innocent people on the altar of nationalism. Another Baez composition, "All the Weary Mothers of the Earth," looks forward to a millenial day when all the mothers, farmers, and workers on earth will rest in a peaceful world. However, her most interesting ballad is "To Bobby," a rather evident though not explicit appeal to Bob Dylan, asking him to rejoin the protest movement. The song accuses Bobby of leaving the protestors "marching on the road" when the struggle was "barely at its start." One line comments that "no one could say it" like Bobby "said it"; the others would just "try and then forget it." The last verse notes that Baez and her compatriots continue to march in the streets "with little victories and big defeats" and still reserve a place for the unidentified Bobby. Rounding out the album songs are Mimi Farina's "In the Quiet Morning," a memorial to Janis Joplin; a World War Two ballad, "The Partisan," here dedicated to Melina Mercouri and those suffering under "the current Greek dictatorship"; and John Lennon's hit, "Imagine," a call for one-world socialism. *Come From the Shadows* is the most explicitly political of Baez's albums, and though it is somewhat gushy and polemic in spots, Joan's own compositions continue the promise of her earlier songs.[28]

Ironically, as Baez has increased the scope and control of her music, her musical identity has become less important. Once she was a pacifist folksinger, now she sees herself as a folksinger pacifist. However, most Americans see Joan as a celebrity. Her celebrity status is evidenced by the regular appearance of her name in the "People" sections of *Newsweek* and *Time* and in daily syndicated gossip columns. It is further evidenced by the balloting for the Playboy Jazz & Pop Hall of Fame. In the latest poll, Joan placed thirteenth, right behind rock-star Frank Zappa and ahead of singer Barbra Streisand.[29] Daniel Boorstin defines a celebrity as "a person who is known for his well-knowness." Unlike the hero who is famous for his deeds, the celebrity is famous for his fame. "The hero was a big man; the celebrity is a big name."[30] Yet, Baez is not a classic celebrity. She was not suddenly created by the media's need for instant cultural heroes. It was her deeds rather than her image that had changed over the years. Baez's celebrity status made her beliefs and actions newsworthy, but her activities usually threatened her professional career.

Moreover, Joan feels celebrities have a responsibility. In 1967 when Bob Dylan was at the height of his popularity, and Baez's career was somewhat in eclipse, Joan noted:

> The kids idealize Dylan more than me. For that reason I think he should help them more, not play up to their negative feelings. What they want to hear is that nothing matters; and in a way that's what his newer songs tell them. I say just the opposite; I believe everything matters, and you have to take a stand.[31]

Unlike Dylan and other rock-stars, Baez had neither the attitudes nor lifestyle to endear her to the counter culture. True, she condoned pre-marital sex and advocated trial marriage (and had practiced both by age 20), but she urged discipline and commitment and was rather puritanical about drugs. In 1968 she admitted a "total dislike" for liquor and cigarettes, as well as marijuana or other drugs. "I get high as a cloud on one sleeping pill," Joan observed, "if that's what it means to get high; and it's not a whole lot different from what I feel like on a fall day in New England, or listening to the Faure Requiem."[32] Also, Baez has steadily drawn criticism from the young Left for her negative attitude toward various black power movements and women's liberation groups. Joan's position is based on the belief that people must concentrate on what they have in common rather than what sets them apart. She feels that power ultimately subverts and corrupts those who gain it. Thus, for Baez, even Martin Luther King's non-violent movement was faulty, since it sought narrow changes by pressuring government. Joan's hero is Gandhi who never asked for power, but "assumed that the power was the people's" and brought change by asking the people, rather than the government, to act.[33]

Not surprisingly, Baez has also been attacked from the Right. For example, in 1966 David Noebel, a fundamentalist minister, charged that Joan's Institute was a marxist-oriented front that trained "muscle-bound toughs" for group disruptions. Noebel also noted that in 1962 the two biggest donors to the United Nations were Nelson Rockefeller and Joan Baez (who gave $1,361.60); and that Joan's Father held "down one of the highest paid jobs in the UNESCO Secretariat."[34] More importantly, in 1967 cartoonist Al Capp introduced a character into his "Li'l Abner" strip named "Joanie Phoanie." Miss Phoanie was a long-haired folksinger who collected $10,000 a concert, refused to pay taxes, and spent most of her spare time organizing sordid, anti-American demonstrations. Joan's defenders pointed out that Capp had made his fortune distorting and maligning the image of Appalachian whites, so his treatment of Baez was a logical extension of his work.[35]

Largely because of the controversy that has surrounded her, Baez has been a cultural hero of youth throughout the decade. Earlier, however, she was only a model of style. Thus, in 1962 *Time* suggested how to look like a female "folknik": "It is not absolutely essential to have hair hanging to the waist—but it helps. Other aids:

no lipstick, flat shoes, a guitar."[36] *Time* really described how to look like Joan Baez. At present, a cursory glance at any group of teenage girls (or perhaps boys also) quickly indicates that the style Baez picked up in the bohemian corners of Harvard, and later helped popularize, is now everywhere triumphant. Millions of youths now dress in long hair and ostentatious poverty. Yet, Joan does not cherish her part in the style revolution, since her message was never explicitly in her lifestyle. As early as 1961, Baez felt that she had "a lot to say," but added: "I don't know how to say it so I just sing it."[37] Later, no doubt, she felt that it was not enough to sing it or say it, so she did it. If Marshal McLuhan is any guide, she is on the right track. For if "the medium is the message," surely the singer must, in part, be the lyrics.

Baez has come a long way intellectually, but her answers to social problems often remain naive, hopeful, and vague (or as social scientists would say, without empirical foundation). Joan probably realizes this much more in her new-found maturity. She has admitted that she cannot explain her "innermost convictions." For her, it is enough to say: "A tree is known by its fruits. People see how I manage myself, and maybe from that they can see what I'm about."[38] Perhaps Joan Baez is a fake—the brainchild of a brilliant public relations man—a pseudo protest singer who chose to become commercial by being non-commercial. Perhaps her activities are really sublimations for personal conflicts she only dimly perceives. Perhaps her vision of a non-violent world is based on untenable assumptions about human nature. In any case, I read the record of her life as indicating that she came by her convictions honestly—indeed, that her beliefs were rationally shaped by her odyssey through the turbulent 1960's.

Baez has clearly been cast in the hero's role. In 1971, for example, in Antioch College's annual poll of their freshmen to determine what prominent persons of recent history the students most admired, Joan Baez placed eleventh—right behind John Kennedy. Women's liberation notwithstanding, she was the first woman on the list. Gandhi ranked first and Martin Luther King second; others among the top ten were Malcolm X, Albert Schweitzer, Ralph Nader, Cesar Chavez, and Pablo Picasso.[39] Baez was indeed in august company. However, perhaps her strong showing was not too surprising. Increasingly, Joan appears wherever the action is. Marching in the streets, on television talk shows, in daily news dispatches, or singing the title song in a movie about Sacco and Vanzetti, she now seems a natural symbol of our era.

Perhaps in no other decade could a female pacifist become a cultural hero, or could a folksinger become a symbol for American youth. Like Joan of Arc, Baez inspired by example and symbolized innocence and purity. For many, Joan Baez fulfilled the perennial quest for an individual pure in heart who could not be bought. Too volatile and profane to be a serious candidate for sainthood, Baez has nevertheless acquired a saintly image. Although she has long since written off the Berkeley Free Speech Movement as an "unviolent" movement (ready to switch to violence to obtain its goals), as opposed to a truly "nonviolent" movement, her part in the Berkeley turmoil was a good example of her charisma. "Have love as you do this thing," Joan told a Berkeley mob, "and it will succeed." Later, *Time* magazine reported that 1,000 undergraduates had "stormed" the administration building "marching behind their Joan of Arc, who was wearing a jeweled crucifix."[40] At first glance it seemed odd to compare the peaceful Baez to the warrior-maid of France; but then Baez does insist on describing herself as a "nonviolent soldier." And on "The Les Crane Show," she had admitted once instructing a crowd of protestors: "Be nonviolent or I'll kill you!" And so I choose to see her as "A Pacifist St. Joan"—on a white horse, without armour, guitar (rather than lance) in hand—riding at the head of a nonviolent army.

NOTES

[1]Her tax protests were only symbolic. The Internal Revenue Department simply attached her bank account and collected not only her total tax bill, but additional penalty interest. For her original reasons for her tax protest, see her letter to The Internal Revenue Service, reprinted in *Sing Out*, 14 (June, 1964), p. 12.

[2]The Institute is now in its seventh year of operation. For a witty look at the early Institute, see Joan Didion, "Just Folks At a School For Nonviolence," *New York Times Magazine*, February 27, 1966.

[3]For biographical data on Baez's early years, most writers rely on *Time*'s research staff. See their feature article on Joan, "Sibyl With Guitar," November 23, 1962, pp. 54-56+. For much more detailed, though incomplete, information, see Joan Baez's semi-autobiographical *Daybreak* (New York, 1968), especially, pp. 1-66.

[4]Interview with Joan Baez, Dan Wakefield, "I'm Really a Square," *Redbook*,

128 (January, 1967), p. 115.

⁵Baez, *Daybreak,* pp. 40, 42, 48-49. Joan added that since 1947, her father "never accepted a job that had anything to do with armaments, offense, defense, or whatever they prefer to call it."

⁶*Ibid.,* p. 40.

⁷"To Prison With Love," *Time* (December 11, 1964), p. 60. Folksinger Phil Ochs was also involved in the Free Speech Movement at Berkeley.

⁸Joan Baez, "With God on Our Side," *Liberation,* 10 (August, 1965), p. 35.

⁹Robert Simple, "Vietnam Critics Stage Sit-Down at White House," *New York Times,* August 7, 1965.

¹⁰Peter Braestrup, "Joan Baez and the Interpreter, or What the Japanese Didn't Hear," *New York Times,* February 21, 1967; Editorial, *Sing Out,* 17, (April, 1967), p. 1.

¹¹Baez, *Daybreak,* pp. 31-35; "Caroling Joan Baez, Mother Arrested at War Protest," UPI dispatch in *Dallas Morning News,* December 20, 1967.

¹²For an account of David and Joan's anti-war activities before he entered prison, see *Daybreak,* pp. 149-157 and Nat Hentoff's excellent "Playboy Interview: Joan Baez," *Playboy,* July, 1970, pp. 54-62+. Also, a documentary film, *Carry It On,* which covered their campus tours in 1968 and 1969 was released in 1970.

¹³"The Dick Cavett Show," August 4, 1969. Howard K. Smith, quoted on "The ABC Evening News," August 5, 1969. Baez's earlier appearances were "The Alan Burke Show," October 28, 1967 and "The Les Crane Show," August 30, 1968. She also was a guest on "The David Frost Show" with son, Gabriel, June 20, 1970. All comments are based on audio tapes of the television shows.

¹⁴Quoted in *Newsweek,* September 14, 1970, p. 65.

¹⁵News story, *Fort Worth Star Telegram,* Feburary 4, 1971.

¹⁶Jack O'Brian, column in *Fort Worth Star Telegram,* February 23, 1971. This had always been a problem when she toured with her husband. Crowds came to hear her sing and were impatient with David's philosophical harangues.

¹⁷Quoted on "The Dick Cavett Show," February 9, 1971 and "The David Frost Show," March 12, 1971.

¹⁸Richard Farina, "Baez and Dylan: A Generation Singing Out," in *The American Folk Scene,* edited by David A. DeTurk and A. Poulin, Jr. (New York, 1967), p. 253. The article was originally printed in *Mademoiselle* in March, 1964.

¹⁹The Institute has regularly announced its activities through a *Newsletter* available on request. Its views are most explicit perhaps in the brief pamphlets

it distributes, such as Emile Copouye, *Laying Down the Gun,* David Harris, *The Big Lie Technique,* and Henry Anderson, *The Denaturization of Human Nature.* On the establishment of the Institute see, David A. DeTurk and A. Poulin, Jr., "Joan Baez: An Interview," in *The American Folk Scene,* pp. 231-249; Baez, *Daybreak,* pp. 56-76.

20David Harris, *Goliath* (New York, 1970).

21Baez, *Daybreak,* p. 136.

22Hentoff, "Playboy Interviews: Joan Baez," p. 54.

23Baez, *Daybreak,* p. 77.

24Paul Nelson and Jon Panake, "Record Reviews," *Little Sandy Review,* 18 (September, 1961), pp. 3-6.

25Alan Weberman and Gordon Friesen, "Joan Baez and the Bob Dylan Songs," *Broadside,* no. 97 (March, 1969), pp. 1-2, 9-10.

26Her early albums (all recorded by Vanguard) were *Joan Baez* (1960), *Joan Baez, Volume 2* (1961), *Joan Baez in Concert* (1962), *Joan Baez in Concert, Part 2* (1962), *Joan Baez 5* (1963), *Farewell Angelina* (1965), and *Noel* (1966).

27Quoted in, Dan Wakefield, "I'm Really a Square," p. 123.

28Her last seven albums on Vanguard were *Joan* (1967), *Baptism* (1968), *Any Day Now* (1969), *David's Album* (1969), *One Day At a Time* (1970), *Joan Baez: The First Ten Years* (1970), and *Blessed Are* (1971). Her last record, *Come From the Shadows,* was recorded and released by A & M Records in 1972.

29Nat Hentoff, "Jazz and Pop '72," *Playboy* (February, 1972), pp. 211-212.

30Daniel J. Boorstin, *The Image: Or What Happened to the American Dream* (New York, 1962), pp. 45-76.

31Quoted in Wakefield, "I'm Really a Square," p. 120.

32Baez, *Daybreak,* pp. 42-44.

33For a typical attack on Baez's view of black power, see the editorial, *Broadside,* no. 83 (August, 1967), pp. 8-9. For her present views on various activist groups, see Hentoff, "Playboy Interview: Joan Baez."

34David A. Noebel, *Rhythm, Riots, and Revolution* (Tulsa, 1966), pp. 202-203.

35Editorial, *Broadside,* no. 79 (February, 1967), p. 2.

36"The Folk Girls," *Time,* June 1, 1962, p. 39.

37"Hoots and Hollers on the Campus," *Newsweek,* November 27, 1961, p. 84.

38Quoted in Tom O'Leary, "Joan Baez—A Lesser Flop," *World Campus,*

2 (December, 1967), p. 15.

[39]Results of the Antioch poll reproduced in *Parade* magazine, May 28, 1972, p. 4. In the 1964 poll Gandhi still ranked first, John Kennedy was second, and though Schweitzer and King were in the top ten, so were Winston Churchill, Franklin Roosevelt, Albert Einstein, and Woodrow Wilson. The only woman on the 1964 list was Eleanor Roosevelt who placed eighth.

[40]"To Prison With Love," p. 60.

By BRUCE LOHOF

The Bacharach Phenomenon

The story is told that in 1943, Burt Bacharach, then a lad of fifteen years, was whistling a tune while a Manhattan bus carried him to his piano lesson.

"Is that 'The Two O'Clock Jump'?" asked a young man seated next to him. He was, it turned out, Leonard Bernstein, assistant conductor of the New York Philharmonic Orchestra.

"I've never heard of you," said the callow Bacharach. But the two young musicians chatted for a while, and when the bus rolled up to Burt's stop, he got off, saying: "So long, Lenny, see you at the top."

This pretentious augury of youth in time became prophecy fulfilled. Leonard Bernstein disembarked from that bus to become conductor of the New York City Symphony and, later, musical director of the New York Philharmonic. He has watched the ballerinas twirl to his *Fancy Free*; he has listened with millions to the music of his Broadway-come-Hollywood hit *West Side Story*; he has seen Marlon Brando mumble and stumble to the accompaniment of his score for *On the Waterfront*. He has become a widely televised lecturer-conductor, an ambassador of classical music to the court of little children, and a tousle-headed symbol of a culture that is not only *haute* but good fun as well. And what of Bacharach? For his part he has become a famous

composer of popular music. More, he has become a national idol.
He is for his time what Stephen Foster, Irving Berlin, George Gershwin,
and Cole Porter were for theirs. He is, as one news magazine put it in
its cover story of him, a "Music Man."[1]

How does a callow lad grow into a Music Man? Composers these
days must sing their own if they would be famous. Moreover, they
must sing them drenched in the day-glo of strobe lights and psychedelia
(e.g., the Beatles and Bob Dylan). The others—Sammy Cahn, Henry
Mancini, et al—continue to receive about as much public acclaim as a
group of certified public accountants. How is it, then, that in this
setting Burt Bacharach, tunesmith, would become a national idol?
What are the contours of the Bacharach phenomenon? And what do
they tell us about the stuff of which popular heroes are made?

That Bacharach is a popular hero is no longer open to question.
Students of hero-worship have long since charted the genetic process
by which heroes are born, and Bacharach has definitely entered the
sequence. Two decades ago Orrin Klapp designated "the main phases
of this process . . . as follows: (1) spontaneous or unorganized popular
homage, (2) formal recognition and honor, (3) the building up of an
idealized image or legend of the hero, (4) commemoration of the hero,
and (5) established cult." Klapp hastened to remind his readers that
all heroes need not pass through the entire sequence.[2] But Bacharach
is already on his way.

Popular homage takes a variety of forms. Charles Lindbergh's
heroism began at Orly Field when thousands of Frenchmen dragged
him bodily from "The Spirit of St. Louis" and carried him upon their
shoulders for nearly a half hour. The heroism of the brothers Kennedy
was born in the frenzied mobs that thronged to touch and see them.
The homage paid to athletes and actors is measured at the box office.
So too, in a manner of speaking, is that paid to Burt Bacharach. At
age forty-two he is, by pecuniary standards, the beneficiary of popular
homage. The people have deigned to turn more than two dozen of his
songs into hits.[3] A single artist, Dionne Warwick, has sold more than
twelve million copies of Bacharach tunes. One of his songs, "Raindrops
Keep Fallin' On My Head," has sold three million recordings and nearly
a million copies of sheet music. Bacharach commands $35,000 per
week for concerts. He owns a lucrative share of the company which
produces his recordings and all of the publishing house that sells his
music. In a land and business where popular homage is gauged in dollars,

Bacharach is a wealthy man.[4]

Formal recognition and honor began in 1970. In March, Bacharach received two "Oscars" from the American Academy of Motion Picture Arts and Sciences, one for the musical score of *Butch Cassidy and the Sundance Kid,* the other for a song from that score, "Raindrops Keep Fallin' On My Head." A month later the National Academy of Recording Arts and Sciences awarded him two "Grammies," one for the score of *Butch Cassidy and the Sundance Kid,* the other for the recorded soundtrack of his Broadway hit, *Promises, Promises.* Continued formal recognition of Bacharach can be confidently predicted.

Following in the train of spontaneous homage and formal recognition—and in keeping with Klapp's sequence of hero-development—is the evolution of a Bacharach *image and legend.* The Bacharach of the flesh is, of course, an unknown quantity. This is true, certainly, of all public figures. But it is doubly true of Bacharach, for his is an occupation that usually dictates obscurity, leaving the limelight to those who perform the music. (It is interesting to note, for example, that Bacharach's lyricist partner Hal David remains a completely obscure figure.) The public's ignorance of the real Bacharach makes the evolution of a consumable Bacharach necessary, for heroes can be mysterious or enigmatic, but never intangible. It also makes such an evolution easy, for little of the real Bacharach exists to erase or contradict.

The consumable Bacharach is partially an image. We know, for instance, that he is erotically handsome. "Burt has turned out to be a sex symbol," producer David Merrick has been quoted as saying.[5] We know also that in matters both tonsorial and sartorial he is impeccably disheveled, studiously unkempt, casually "in." Still another part of the image looms large in his concerts, live or televised: the calisthenic nature of his musical conducting style, complete with karate chops to the percussion section, blurring fingers in the direction of the woodwinds, lightning body swivels from one piano to another. Each of these pieces of the Bacharach image is, moreover, caught in the stop-action portrait that image makers have used as a signature for his televised concerts.[6] The erotic good looks, the tousled hair and casual clothing, the calisthenics—all of it is there, captured forever like the maiden running across Keat's Grecian urn.

But the consumable Bacharach is also partially legend. And the

Bacharach legend, like all heroic epics, takes a familiar form. We nod in recollection at the Alger-come-vaudeville flavor of Bacharach's odyssey in the borscht circuit. Working in a Catskills hotel with a quintet for forty dollars a week (for the quintet, that is), sleeping bunkhouse-style in a chicken shack across the road from the hotel. "We couldn't go home," the legendary Bacharach remembers. "The city meant polio in those days. We were like prisoners. One morning we woke up to fire engines. The hotel had burned down. We cheered."[7] Surprise and then reassurance rolls over us as we discover that Bacharach's Penelope is Angie Dickinson the actress. We knew and loved her when he was Mr. Angie Dickinson, "Magic Moments" was a Perry Como song, and Gene Pitney was singing "The Man Who Shot Liberty Valance." Finally, we thrill to the revelation that Bacharach has been an arranger and accompanist for Vic Damone, the Ames Brothers, Steve Lawrence, and most important, Marlene Dietrich. Dietrich, of course, is more than a hero; she is a goddess. And Bacharach's intimacies with her constitute an important part of the Bacharach legend. Like Odysseus before him, whose mythic sponsor was Athene, Bacharach has been touched by the Olympians. "She's the most generous and giving woman I know," he has said of Dietrich. "If I had a cold she'd swamp me with vitamin C. She once pulverized six steaks for their juice to give me energy. She used to wash my shirts."[8] Could Odysseus have said as much? Bacharach still wears a talisman around his neck as a sign of his Olympian connections: a Dior plaid mohair scarf some twelve feet long. The scarf was given to him by Dietrich while he accompanied her on the international concert stage. "When I arrived in Poland to meet Marlene, she was waiting for me, in a snowstorm, at the airport with this scarf, so I'd be warm." Attesting to the acceptance of the talisman, Bacharach has said: "I can't wear bizarre clothes . . . but anything Marlene gave me always felt sensible and right."[9]

The consumable Bacharach, then, exists. Partly image and partly legend, it qualifies as fulfillment of Klapp's third criterion of American heroes. What of the final criterion, commemoration and cult establishment? Already Bacharach fan clubs have begun. But history, the fans, and Bacharach will have to wait. Total heroism, one suspects, will come only after a fiery death by automobile (a la James Dean) or airplane (a la Will Rogers), followed—after a respectable period of mourning—by the issuance of a commemorative stamp. Bacharach is doubtless reluctant to follow through. In any case, Klapp insists that it is not mandatory. Bacharach is already a heroic figure, born of genetic processes with which hero-watchers are familiar.

If the Bacharach phenomenon mirrors a generic form of hero-making, it also mirrors a generic form of hero-being, for the constituent parts of Bacharach's hero status are typical of heroism generally. For instance:

Hero-making situations.[10] Heroes, like bacteria, live best in congenial environments. The hero's Petri dish may be a grand political or military crisis, some stupendous scientific achievement, a mere theatrical or sporting event. Indeed, any situation is hero-making if it focuses public attention upon some unmet need. Burt Bacharach lives in such an environment. The world of popular music receives a constant glare from the public eye. Americans spend more than a billion dollars annually on recorded popular music. The demand for popular tunes is insatiable, the locale ubiquitous. Moreover, Americans have what Daniel Boorstin calls "extravagant expectations" with respect to music (and everything else). The music must not only keep coming, it must be original and stimulating. The latest tune must also be the greatest tune.[11] The composer becomes Sisyphus in a spotlight, forever rolling his rock through the glare of public attention toward an unmet need. His situation is truly heroic.

Heroic role. But situation does not a hero make. He must rise to the occasion by fulfilling one of many heroic roles. He must become a conquering hero (Beowulf or Babe Ruth) or a Cinderella (David [of David-and-Goliath] or Charles Lindbergh), a clever hero whose brains triumph over brawn (Br'er Rabbit), an avenging hero (James Bond), a benefactor (Robin Hood), or a martyr (Joan of Arc).[12] Bacharach's manner is too soft for him to play the conqueror, too shy to play the avenger. Nor is he a man given to beneficence or martyrdom. Like many American heroes—molded as they are in the Algeresque tradition —Bacharach is a Cinderella, a "dark horse" who has made good. His legend fits the typical pattern: obscure origins, "instant" success in his late thirties after decades of hard work and meager rewards.[13] Even in success he is the Cinderella man surmounting adversity. Legend has it that when *Promises, Promises* was in Boston preparing for Broadway it was decided that another song would be needed. Bacharach— haggard from a bout with pneumonia that had put him into the hospital

—and David wrote the song in a single day. It entered the show immediately. Sick men do not write good songs in a single day. But heroes do. The tune—"I'll Never Fall in Love Again"—was later recorded by Dionne Warwick and spent eleven weeks on the hit record charts.[14]

"Color." "The quality of 'color,' " says Klapp, "seems to be in actions or traits which excite popular interest and imagination."[15] "Color" is a paler shade of charisma, and heroes—Bacharach included —have it. "Color" is Muhammad Ali's circling style of pugilism and his doggerel style of poetry. "Color" is the way John Kennedy said "viga'," the way Bobby nervously fought his tousled locks, and the way every Kennedy played touch football. "Color" exudes also from the properties of heroes: Roosevelt's cigaret holder and Churchill's cigar, King Arthur's Excalibur and Patton's pearl-handled pistols, Christ's seamless robe and Linus's filthy blanket. Bacharach's "color" is, of course, found in his image and legend. His handsome features, his clothing, his style of musical conducting, the stories which surround him—all lend that necessary ingredient to the heroism of Burt Bacharach.

But Bacharach's most precious and "colorful" possession is his music. "There are times," an official Bacharach biography says, "when a valuable suggestion is dropped into the mind of a budding composer that remains with him. . . . Burt Bacharach . . . has never forgotten the advice of one of his music tutors, 'Don't be afraid of writing something people can remember and whistle.' "[16] This is a curious anecdote to find in a Bacharach publicity packet, for Bacharach songs cannot be whistled by the man in the street. Indeed, many professional performers sing his music only with great difficulty.[17] His songs are complex and sophisticated. Most popular music is written to formula —3/4 or 4/4 time, 8-bar phrases and a 32-bar song. This fact explains the popular composer's ability to meet the outrageous demands of an insatiable listening public.

But Bacharach rejects such formulae. Regular rhythms seem to bore him. In one passage of "Promises, Promises," for instance, he moves from 3/4 time to 4/4, 3/4, 5/4, 3/4, 4/4, 6/4, 3/4, 4/4, 6/4, 3/4, 3/8, 4/8, 4/4, 5/4, and back to 3/4. For toe-tappers the results are discouraging; they are also exciting and unpredictable. Nor does Bacharach suffer from the 8-to-the-bar syndrome. Some of his music —e.g., "Are You There (With Another Girl)," written in 6-bar phrases—

is orthodox but unconventional. Other songs, such as "The Look of Love" and "I Say a Little Prayer," pretend orthodoxy, but a rambunctious urgency punctuates them with an occasional measure of 2/4 time. Still other pieces are written with formal rhythms, but only, it would seem, to keep the band together. The phrases, musical and lyric, have patterns and pulses of their own. Listen, for example, to "A House Is Not a Home," "The Windows of the World," or "Make It Easy on Yourself." Phrasing dictates rhythm, not vice versa, as is the case in formulaic tunes.[18] And there are other idiosyncrasies. Music critic Charles Champlin has said it well: "He has a way of doing unconventional things with time, with the length of a phrase, with chord patterns and the logic by which one note follows another."[19] There is, in short, a Bacharachian flavor to his music, a distinctive spirit which, without making them all sound alike, stamps each of his songs with the Bacharach mark. And the musical mark is, of course, part of the Bacharach "color." To think of him without his music is to see him in two dimensions, without his graying temples, his soft voice, his Dietrich scarf. To watch and hear Bacharach performing his music is to see him literally in living "color."

Personal traits. Klapp has written that the personal habits and characteristics of heroes are relatively unimportant to their heroism. "Distance," he says, "builds the 'great man,'" and distance stands as a buffer between the intimacies of the hero from the curiosities of his worshipful millions.[20] Still, any personal traits which an attentive public is able to perceive may abet the hero's greatness, especially when they are consistent with the heroic role he has taken and the "color" which cloaks him. Babe Ruth, whose heroism grew from his baseball bat, was the more awesome a figure after scientists proved his eye-hand coordination to be superior to that of most humans. Such is also the case with Bacharach. To the extent that we know the Bacharach of the flesh, we find him consistent with the consumable Bacharach.

We know, for instance, that he is a tireless musician consumed by his work. Each of his television programs gives us a glimpse of his working day—the creation, movieola at his side, of a motion picture score; the production, Dionne Warwick at his side, of another hit record. We know him to be a perfectionist who drives his musicians like a plantation overseer drives his slaves; and we know (or at least we've been told) that they dote upon him in spite of it. It is important that heroes be dedicated to the root base of their fame, and Bacharach is dedicated to his music.

But we know also something of his private life. His marriage to Angie Dickinson, and their daughter, Lea Nikki, born in 1967, contribute substantially to his heroism. Bacharach is everyman, writ large. Like us, he has a family, but it is a hero's family, made of finer stuff. We know also that the Bacharachs live in a luxurious but rented home in Beverly Hills. Nothing could be more proper. It may be well for ancient heroes to reside in temples of stone. Their world is static. But the world of popular music is a popping, whirling scene. Action is its essence. Thus the sumptuous but rented temple is appropriate to its great man. "I'm an impatient man," says Bacharach. "I go one month at a time. That's why Angie and I rent the house. I couldn't wait for one to get built."[21]

So it is that a tunesmith becomes a popular hero. Popular homage turns into formal recognition. Image and legend is constructed, commemorated, and cultified. So it is that a tunesmith stays a hero. A hero-making situation, a heroic role, "color," and compatible personal traits—this is hero stuff. Moreover, this is hero stuff for great men both popular and classical, for Beowulf and Mickey Mouse, Christ and Kennedy.

Still, there is a crucial distinction. Popular heroes are not classical heroes. Peanuts is not Achilles. Greta Garbo was an awesome hero, but no more. Her heroism, like the heroism of all popular idols, was but an eyeblink as compared to the history of the Odysseus cult. Popular heroes are different from classical heroes, and the distinction is symbolized by Bacharach's rented mansion in Beverly Hills. Bacharach is a rented hero. Like Bacharach, the millions who heroize him are impatient men who "go one month at a time." They, too, live in a popping, whirling scene. The man who would be smitten by their worship must be a moving target.

Until yesterday humankind lived in an arrested, static world. To be heroic in the eyes of the ancients was to personify the values of an arrested culture. But the pace of change has accelerated. To an ancient hero, to *stand* for something, is, in our electronic universe, to be obsolete. To be a man for all seasons is to be old-style. Modern heroes last one season at most. To be a newstyle hero is not to *stand* for something, but to *move* for something. Bacharach is a newstyle hero in a newstyle world. The Bacharach phenomenon is a study in motion, a reflection of the frenetic nature of time since yesterday. Bacharach is a popular hero, finally, because he is a moving hero.

NOTES

[1]Hubert Saal, "Burt Bacharach, The Music Man 1970," *Newsweek,* June 22, 1970, pp. 50-54.

[2]Orrin E. Klapp, "Hero Worship in America," *American Sociological Review,* XIV (February, 1949), p. 54. See also Klapp, *Heroes, Villians, and Fools* (Englewood Cliffs, 1962).

[3]Among Bacharach's hit songs are: "Any Day Now," "Tower of Strength," "You're Following Me," "The Man Who Shot Liberty Valance," "Magic Moments," "Don't Make Me Over," "Make It Easy on Yourself," "Only Love Can Break a Heart," "Blue on Blue," "True Love Never Runs Smooth," "24 Hours from Tulsa," "Anyone Who Had a Heart," "Wishin' and Hopin'," "Walk on By," "Reach Out for Me," "I Wake up Cryin'," "Don't Envy Me," "(There's) Always Something There to Remind Me," "Trains and Boats and Planes," "What the World Needs Now is Love," "The Windows of the World," "I Say a Little Prayer," "Raindrops Keep Fallin' on My Head," "I'll Never Fall in Love Again," "Wives and Lovers," "A House is Not a Home," "Send Me No Flowers," "What's New, Pussycat," and "Alfie." See American Society of Composers, Authors and Publishers, *The ASCAP Biographical Dictionary of Composers, Authors, and Publishers,* 3rd ed. (New York, 1966), pp. 26-27.

[4]Data are from Saal, pp. 50, 53.

[5]Quoted in *ibid.,* p. 50.

[6]The stop-action image first appeared in "An Evening with Burt Bacharach," *Kraft Music Hall,* N.B.C. Television, 1970, and reappeared in "Another Evening with Burt Bacharach," *Kraft Music Hall,* N.B.C. Television, 1970.

[7]Quoted in Saal, p. 52.

[8]Quoted in *ibid.,* p. 53.

[9]Quoted in "Composer in Tartan Cap," *The New Yorker,* 44 (December 21, 1968), p. 27.

[10]This and other characteristics of heroes mentioned below are discussed in Orrin E. Klapp, "The Creation of Popular Heroes," *American Journal of Sociology,* LIV, (September, 1948), pp. 135-41.

[11]See Daniel J. Boorstin, *The Image: A Guide to Pseudo-Events in America* (New York, 1961), pp. 3-6, 171-78.

[12]See Klapp, "Creation of Popular Heroes," pp. 136-37.

[13]Leo Lowenthal's content analysis of 168 popular biographies found "hardship" antedating success in so many careers that the "troubles and difficulties with which the road to success is paved are discussed in the form of stereotypes. Over and over again we hear that the going is rough and hard. . . . Defeat or

stalemate [are reported] in matter-of-fact tone, rather than [as] descriptions of life processes." "Biographies in Popular Magazines," in William Peterson, ed., *American Social Patterns* (Garden City, 1956), pp. 93-94.

14Saal, p. 53; "Composer in Tartan Cap," p. 27.

15Klapp, "Creation of Popular Heroes," p. 137.

16[A & M Records], "Burt Bacharach (A Biography)," (mimeograph press release, Hollywood, n.d.).

17Saal quotes Warwick: "You've practically got to be a music major to sing Bacharach;" and Polly Bergen: "I did 'A House Is Not A Home' recently— a great song. But I never did get the timing. I made them write it so I could end up with the band—regardless of how I got lost along the way, and did I ever." p. 51.

18For the sake of convenience, all of these examples are drawn from two albums: *Burt Bacharach: Reach Out* (A & M 131) and *Burt Bacharach: Make It Easy on Yourself* (A & M SP4188). Bacharach composed, arranged, and conducted all of the music on these albums.

19Liner notes for *Burt Bacharach: Make It Easy on Yourself.*

20Klapp, "Creation of Popular Heroes," p. 138.

21Quoted in Saal, p. 54.

PRESIDENT

By DAVID STUPPLE
A Hero for the Times

This is the story of a small time metropolitan businessman who, in the course of five years of saturation advertising on television, became not only an economic success but, more interestingly, a popular hero—one of Detroit's four or five top celebrities. M. J. Lezell, owner of a small but growing home remodeling firm, took his advertising message from the radio and put it on T.V. The results were astonishing. The message was trust, honesty, and sincerity. His slogan was "have no fear." As "Mr. Belvedere, President of the Belvedere Home Construction Company," Lezell (with a little help from his friends and relatives) did his own commercials, exhibited them mercilessly before late night movie audiences, and revolutionized Detroit television advertising. Belvedere construction developed into a major business, extending its market out past Detroit's black ghetto into the suburbs.

While business boomed, the character "Mr. Belvedere" slowly became a *cause celebre*. In the beginning, small pockets of people clustered around T.V. sets waiting for Mr. Belvedere to make his nocturnal visits (he might appear five to six times during the late and the late-late night movie). These "Belvedere freaks" (as they came to be known in the course of our research[1]) found humor in what they considered low-budget, "hoaky" commercials with contrived sets, stumbling performances and trite dialogue. In one classic commercial, recreation room came out as "receration room" and in another, a "telephone operator" did a classic double-take after giving her ten second performance.

The Belvedere freaks cut out pictures of Mr. Belvedere from newspaper ads; some carried the pictures around in billfolds. The pictures showed the somber Mr. Belvedere dressed in a conservative suit with a tidy short haircut, sitting behind a desk with a sign announcing that he was "President"; holding an official looking paper in one hand and pointing authoritatively with the other. This was BUSINESS MAN. You knew he meant it. You knew he meant business.

After two years of this action, a popular radio disc jockey began to make playful parodies of the Belvedere commercials. A newspaper facetiously awarded Belvedere the "President's Cup," and asked readers "Do you fear this man?" The fad grew. Folksingers included the company's commercial jingle in their repertoires. Fan letters, requests for autographed pictures and for fan club materials trickled into the Belvedere construction office.

Promotional materials proliferated. Included were Belvedere T-shirts, night-shirts, posters, bumper-stickers, buttons, ink pens, windshield scrapers, balloons, a phonograph record, fan club cards and a helicopter that trailed a sign urging sightseers to "have no fear with Belvedere."

Mr. Belvedere began making public appearances. He appeared in a float in the State Fair Parade, "stole the show" from Buffalo Bob and Howdy Doody at a Civic benefit, appeared on fund raising programs for muscular distrophy, the March of Dimes, educational television, the United Fund, the State of Israel and an inner-city mission. He played with children on the Bozo the Clown T.V. show, judged a dance contest, judged a twin contest, threw out "the first ball" to the mayor of Detroit in a mock opening day baseball ceremony. He spoke to college audiences. He m.c.'d a music concert (where he awarded T-shirt prizes to those who could sing his jingle, the "magic number song," without laughing). He let his hair grow and did openly camp commercials.

Thousands of T-shirts and posters were sold. His birthday was celebrated at the University of Michigan. A mysterious Belvedere "look-alike" caused a minor sensation by impersonating Belvedere on the stage of suburban night spots.

A new trend in Detroit television advertising developed. A public utility, a funeral home, an automobile dealer, a home appliance chain store, a hi fi equipment dealer and others produced advertisements patterned after the Belvedere model.

Rumors spread. Who were the people who performed on his commercials? Is it true that he doesn't own a business at all but only farms out the work to "real" construction companies? Did he appear on a radio talk show and suggest that potential customers take some of their problem work to competitors who specialized in certain jobs? Was the money he made from the T-shirts and posters going to charity? Was he going to run around the streets of Detroit in a gorilla suit to support the March of Dimes?

Heroes reflect their times. As one observer has pointed out, they must act their ages. In the Middle Ages, heroes were God's men; in the nineteenth century, self-made men; and in the twentieth century, common men and the outsiders.[2] In the period after World War II, the common man—the anti-hero—has been joined by the *camp hero*. Mr. Belvedere is a massively beautiful example of this new breed.

But what is a camp hero and how does one become a camp hero? By doing some reflection on these questions and taking the case of Mr. Belvedere, we can make some inquiries into the character of contemporary urban American society.

Television

The key to success for Mr. Lezell *and* Mr. Belvedere is television. Lezell had similar advertisements on the radio for five previous years. While business grew, it was nothing like what happened when he began on T.V.

Following McLuhan, we may observe that Mr. Belvedere presented a hot message on a cool medium. Belvedere's voice was strident and the message emphatic. Some commercials featured a gaudy flashing neon sign pointing the way to the Belvedere office.

Furthermore, Mr. Belvedere's demeanor and his setting were incongruent with his message of trust and integrity. The actors in the Belvedere commercials gave off the impression of being indiscreet, immodest and as having faulty control over speech and physical movements. They simply did not pull it off.[3]

The Camp Sensibility

The artistic failure described above is not so bad if you want to become a camp hero. The fact is that Lezell had no intention of becoming a camp hero. He simply wanted to put his message across man-to-man. Straight arrow. Again, this was fortuitous because *pure camp* is always *innocent.*

Passmore puts it this way:

> A thing is camp if it has serious intent, but fails in some
> seriously interesting way.

and that

> Deadpan seriousness that fails, contrivence, anachronism,
> stereotyping and exaggeration are the hallmarks of camp.[4]

Sontag makes the following observations that apply to the Belvedere phenomenon:

> Pure Camp is always naive . . . when something is just bad
> (rather than Camp), it's often because it is too mediocre in
> its ambition . . . the whole point of camp is to dethrone the
> serious. Camp is playful, anti-serious . . . camp appreciates
> vulgarity . . . what [camp] does is to find success in certain
> passionate failures. Camp taste is a kind of love, love for
> human nature. It relishes rather than judges . . . camp taste
> identifies with what it is enjoying . . . camp is a tender feeling.[5]

A camp hero then, is a loser that becomes a winner. He is celebrated and appreciated for his faults. A camp hero becomes the object of a tolerant and sweet cynicism. This distinguishes him from a mock hero who is genuinely ridiculed. Mock heroes apparently appear in many epochs, while the camp hero is a contemporary figure.

The Mr. Belvedere phenomenon would never have developed without television nor would it have developed without the concurrent development of the camp aesthetic. The nature of television rendered Mr. Belvedere's heroic stance and his heroic message enjoyably absurd.

In closing, we point out that the fad would not have reached its mature form without the availability of T-shirting, postering, buttoning and bumper sticking as vehicles for the articulation and spread of public opinion. Similarly, the new style radio disc jockey played an integral role in the public career of Mr. Belvedere. Each of these culture traits is worthy of its own investigation in the study of the development of popular culture.

NOTES

[1] Research for this article included interviews with M. J. Lezell and his associates conducted in various situations and under various circumstances. Also included were both "quick and dirty," and in-depth interviews with his public—again conducted in various situations and circumstances. A number of newspaper articles about the Belvedere phenomenon appeared in Detroit area papers and were helpful in the research. I am indebted to many interested parties, particularly Barbara Stevens, for their suggestions, criticisms, and collection of data.

[2] Marshall Fishwick. *The Hero: American Style.* New York: Van Rees Press, 1969. P. 5.

[3] See Erving Goffman, *The Presentation of Self in Everyday Life.* New York: Doubleday & Co., 1959.

[4] John Passmore, "Camp Style in Ekwenski" in Marshall Fishwick (ed.) *Remus, Rastus, Revolution.* Bowling Green, Ohio: Bowling Green State University, Popular Press, 1971. Pp. 100-101.

[5] Susan Sontag, "Notes on Camp" in *Against Interpretation*, New York: Farrar, Strauss & Grioux, 1961.

By JOHN STEVENS
The Dog as Hero

If, as has often been asserted, no man is a hero to his valet, then probably it is equally true that no man is a hero to his dog. The dog, like the valet, sees the man in all his moods and in all his unguarded moments. Man worries less about the dog than the valet because the dog cannot talk; perhaps it is for that reason that man has been so willing to make the dog a heroic character in much of his popular culture. Then again, maybe it is as a bribe to keep dogs from learning to talk.

One reason men have elevated canines to Valhalla in songs, movies, radio serials, television series and comic strips is that dogs are *there*, and in great profusion. Almost everyone has owned or loved a dog. On the other hand, there are more cats than dogs, and the cat has not fared nearly so well in the popular arts. Cats are seen as intelligent, but aloof and sneaky. Dogs are considered warm, loyal, intuitive and physically powerful—the stuff of which any hero is made.

The dog is a convenient symbol for whatever a man wants to make of him. For youth in the counter-culture, dogs are free spirits. They keep them in their houses and apartments as convenient love objects which demand little in return. For their parents, dogs may either be a possession or a protector of their person or possessions.

Even our idiomatic expressions are both derogatory (dog tired, doggone, a dog's life) and favorable (gay dog, putting on the dog). "Dog" in the sense of untiring pursuit is favorable but in the sense of an inferior product is the opposite.

There are dogs in folk music, but one must look to commercial country music for dog heroes. There you will find a pack of Old Dog Trays and Blues, usually aging hounds who have shared hunting joys with their masters. In at least one such song, we are assured that if dogs go to Heaven (and surely they must) then this one will be there a'waiting. More recently, Johnny Cash introduced an anti-hero, *That Dirty Old Egg-Sucking Dog*.

Dogs have been a staple of adventure fiction, particularly children's stories, for a long time. Tales of huskies rushing the serum to Nome or of St. Bernards rescuing injured skiers in the Alps are legion. So are stories about faithful dog companions and brave guardians.

There have been canine heroes in the movies almost from the beginning. Vitagraph had the first, Jean. The beautiful collie was an established star by 1911 and one of the few actors whose name was known to the public. Early moviemakers did not name their cast members for fear they would get a star complex and demand more money; when they finally acceded to the public's demands for names, their early fears proved well-founded. It was said that Jean did no "tricks"; she only acted. Among the dozens of short films in which she appeared, several included her name in the title, such as *Jean the Matchmaker* and *Jean Goes Foraging*. When she returned to the cameras after a maternity leave, the Vitagraph directors worked her pups into some movies.[1]

Perhaps the greatest dog hero of them all in the motion pictures was Rin-Tin-Tin. An American army sergeant found the police dog behind the lines in France during World War I, brought him home with him and trained him. Rin-Tin-Tin made his debut at Warner Brothers in 1923 and became an immediate hit. Five generations of Rin-Tin-Tins appeared in 22 feature films and an early TV serial.[2]

There was nothing passive about Jean or Rin-Tin-Tin. They sensed danger long before the humans and used their barks (sometimes indicated by redundant title cards as "Bow-Wow!") to summon them to the scene of some impending disaster. These dogs often captured desperadoes by holding them at bay with angry snarls or by actually pouncing on them. The races against time (such as summoning aid for a girl tied to railroad tracks) was a real speciality, since it fit into the classic chase pattern of the movies.

Lassie's discovery is every bit as Hollywoodish as Lana Turner's alleged discovery in a corner drugstore; it may be as mythical. As Bosley Crowther tells the story, at least, MGM had assigned the filming of the classic book, *Lassie Come Home*, to its "low budget unit." The producer announced a "mass interview" for a Los Angeles stadium, but he found no dog to his liking from among the hundreds who showed up. He then instructed a professional dog trainer to scour the country for likely collies and bring them back for screen tests. He showed up with a truckload, but none seemed right. Then the producer noticed a year-old male still in the truck. The trainer explained that was his own dog, Pal, one he had picked up a few months before as a cull from a litter in lieu of a $10 debt. In true Hollywood fashion, that dog was cast in the title role, and as the saying goes, the rest is history.[3] The dog was not the only one to make a debut in that 1943 movie: there also was a strikingly beautiful little 10-year-old brunette named Elizabeth Taylor. Lassie, *nee* Pal, was a remarkable animal, both smart and affectionate. He played in all future Lassie pictures until his son, Laddie, could take over for him when *Lassie* became a television serial.

Studio soundmen made many a dog whimper or bark beside its master in the days of radio serials. The only canine hero to rate his own show was Yukon King.

Young Sergeant Preston saved the husky pup from an attack by a marauding lynx. ("I'm going to call you Yukon King. I'll teach you self-control, and how to best use your great strength. Youngster, we're going to be partners. And when you're grown, you are going to be the greatest dog in the Yukon!")

Preston and King became the same kind of champions of justice that the Lone Ranger and Tonto became. That is not too surprising, since they were the products of the same producer, director and more often even the same cast from the same station, Detroit's WXYZ. More than once, they performed only slightly refurbished Ranger scripts.

Jim Harmon, in his book on old-time radio, illustrates King's role with this passage:[4]

PRESTON: I'm going to have to ride to the Fort for help . . .
KING: Grrrr-bow-wow-wow! Rruff!
PRESTON: Yes, King—What is it, boy?
KING: Bow-wow-wow!
PRESTON: He's trying to tell me something . . . Yes, King?
KING: Rruff! Bow-wow! Rruff!
PRESTON: He's saying . . . he should go in my place. I
should stay here. You're right, King!

George W. Trendle was the creator not only of The Lone Ranger and Yukon King, but also the Green Hornet. He sold the rights to the Ranger after making 52 shows himself for $3,650,000 in 1952. He collected $1.5 million for the rights to Yukon King in 1957, and his estate still owns the Green Hornet.

NBC-TV produced Yukon King for five years, and it still is showing in syndication. Trendle was a consultant on the TV series, and in 1969 he recalled some of the problems with the show. First, it took months to find and train the right dog for the part of King. Then one day a stage hand put too much grease in a cabin for a fire scene and King singed his hind quarters and refused to act. Another time a director thought King should look wet after apparently jumping into a creek and soused him with cold water. "He was a very temperamental actor," Trendle recalled.[5]

In New York, at least, there were specialists in the sounds of animals who went from radio show to theater, imitating all manner of birds and beasts, including many dogs. Some were purists, insisting on reproducing the sounds by means of their vocal cords alone, while others used mechanical aids.[6]

Most of the dogs who "appeared" on the radio programs were not, of course, heroes; rather, they were incidental characters. Some of these dogs appeared regularly, such as Asta on The Thin Man or Daisy on the Blondie show.

For obvious reasons, dogs have been relatively rare as stage stars. In broadcasting or in the movies, shots can be taken again and again until they are right, but on the stage, there is only one chance at each performance. Few dogs can perform more than the most routine action on cue, but sometimes they play important—if small—parts in stage productions such as The Miracle Worker. One of the few dogs to get its name in the title of a stage production was Sheba in Come Back Little Sheba.

Walt Disney's animators created a number of memorable dogs,

such as Pluto; however, Pluto was confined mostly to short cartoons. At least two of Disney's animated features, *Lady and the Tramp* and *One Hundred and One Dalmations* focused primarily on canines. He used life actors and dogs to bring to the screen such classics as *Greyfriars Bobby* and *Dog of Flanders*.

Except for Pluto, there have been few dog heroes in animated cartoons, although bulldogs portray authority figures for Tweetie Pie ("I tot I saw a puddy tat") and for Jerry in his eternal feud with Tom. Here the bird and mouse use the dog's natural animosity toward the cat to their own advantage.

Manfred "the wonder dog"—a longtime staple cartoon feature on Captain Kangaroo—is sort of an anti-hero. Tom Terrific is always breathlessly proclaiming Manfred's virtues, but Manfred mostly sleeps. Tom will ask him something and Manfred will mutter, "Huh?" which Tom then interprets as the wisdom of the ages. ("Manfred, you've done it again!")

The changing role of the dog as hero is even better illustrated in the newspaper comic strip. On February 16, 1896, readers of the New York Sunday *World* found a panel drawing which filled most of one page. It was entitled "The Great Dog Show in M'Googan's Avenue" and was signed "Outcault." A bunch of slum kids were all dressed up and showing off their pets. Right in the middle was a weird-looking urchin wearing a bright, yellow flour sack.

Historians usually point out the significance of the event either in terms of the introduction of the Yellow Kid (who became such a sensation that he was stolen back and forth between Hearst and Pulitzer and gave his name to Yellow Journalism) or of technology, since it was a pioneering use of color printing in the newspaper.[7] But it is interesting to note the panel featured dogs.

The earliest known drawings by men, painted on the walls of Paleolithic caves, featured animals. That is not surprising, considering how closely man's life was tied to that of animals. But as Maurice Horn pointed out recently, the comics lineage cannot be traced to such drawings since it was only after the Renaissance that there developed a methodical search for a new medium to combine narrative and picture.[8]

Anthropologists say the dog was domesticated in Europe 20,000 to 25,000 years ago. The folktales of all people emphasize the intelligence and mystery of the dog. Myths about dogs guarding the entrances to the underworld are universal. So is the enmity between dog and cat.[9]

A bunch of loveable animals were rollicking through James Swinnerton's newspaper cartoon, "Little Bears and Tigers" at least four years before the birth of the Yellow Kid; however Swinnerton used his cast in various combinations, while Outcault kept the same central figure.

Coulton Waugh has called animal comics "probably the most important thread in comic-strip history."[10]

Psychologists have written extensively about the egocentric or animistic stage of child development, when the child projects his experiences on many selves. He can be an animal, another person, a giant or a dwarf at will. Often he chooses to be a dog, the animal with which he is most familiar and has most intimate contact around the house.

Although the usual psychological explanation for this stage is that the child is still unable to differentiate himself and these other selves, some researchers on use of the comics have disputed this conclusion. For example, Katherine M. Wolf and Marjorie Fiske said children who preferred animal comics and identified closely with the characters in them did not do so because they were confused; after all, they pointed out their interviewees (all children of the same general age) had no trouble distinguishing themselves from Superman and other superheroes. The real reason, they said, was that the child "has a basic need to constantly enrich his fantasy life with characters."[11]

The comics' first major canine figure was Tige, the bulldog side-kick of Buster Brown. Tige actually debuted in 1897 with the Yellow Kid, but when Outcault traded the urchin in the yellow chemise in for the kid in the Lord Fauntleroy clothes, Tige became a permanent fixture. Not only did Tige talk, he walked on his hind legs. This type of anthropomorphism was far ahead of its time, as we shall see. Although the strip disappeared about World War I, Buster and Tige were salvaged for later generations, mainly through ads for a shoe manufacturer.

Most continuing canine characters were relegated to second-banana spots. This includes the hundreds of assorted mutts who barked their ways through such kid strips as "Reg'lar Fellers" and "Skippy." Rare exceptions included "Wags, the Dog that Adopted a Man," which William F. Marriner drew weekly from 1904 to 1914;

"Cap Stubbs and Tippy," which came along only a bit later, and "Napoleon" who got higher billing than Uncle Elby during the 1930's and 1940's. Today there are "Marmaduke" and "Rivets."

Superheroes have had their animal sidekicks, too. "Ace the Bat Hound" flew with Batman and "Streak the Wonder Dog" with the Green Lantern for many years, and Superman comics were infested with the likes of "Krypto," a flying canine, "Streaky," a flying cat, "Superhorse," "Supermonkey" and even a super-amoeba named "Proty."

So far, we have been discussing only comic strips which feature human beings. In those populated entirely by animals (such as "Peter Rabbit," "The Pussycat Princess," and "Pogo") it is easy to accept their talking and wearing clothes. It does not strike anyone as strange that Mickey Mouse has a pet dog.

Then there was Offissa Pupp, the authority figure in the beloved "Krazy Kat" strip. He spent his career (1911-44) trying to prevent Ignatz Mouse from "kreasing the bean" of poor Krazy with a brick. Like the other characters in the strip, Pupp spoke some wild dialect, the origins of which were known only to George Herriman (and perhaps to his analyst, if he had one).

One of the most interesting dogs in comics history was Gorgon, the high-brow hound in "Barnaby." Not only could he talk, but he delighted in telling shaggy dog stories. The Crockett Johnson fantasy strip, one of the few to feature a leprechaun, graced *PM* and a few other papers during the 1940's.

Clearly the primary role of dogs in comic strips has been to serve as a foil for their masters, usually child heroes. No clearer example exists than Sandy.

In her earliest days, Orphan Annie was much more pathetic. Artist Harold Gray had her talk to the readers through conversations with her doll, Emily Marie, and her dog, Sandy. Somewhere along the line, the doll disappeared. Sandy, a mutt of questionable lineage, has eyeballs as vacant as those of his never-aging mistress. He knows his place. His literal place is on all-fours at Annie's side; his figurative one is to look on, and utter a single syllable when spoken to. No Rin-Tin-Tin, Sandy seldom nips or even growls at any of his mistress' many menacers, nor does he apply his cunning (if he has any) to capture the bad guys. Mostly he listens to Annie's thoughts. ("It was awful dark and spooky on th' road up here from th' village—but everything'll be all right now—there's a light inside—Come on, Sandy!")

In a sample of 838 strips from the 1930's and 1940's, Sandy appeared in 297 (35.4%), but usually he was in the background. He was mentioned by name or addressed directly in only 59 of the strips. He uttered his famous "Arf!" in only 30 strips (3.5%), and then usually when spoken to. ("We'll sit tight and see what happens, eh, Sandy?" "Arf!").

Hardly more communicative than Sandy, but more germane to the plot of its strip, is Daisy. "Blondie" began in 1930 with Dagwood, heir to the Bumstead fortune, courting a Dumb-Dora flapper. When they were married in 1933, Dagwood's family cut him off without a cent, and the Bumsteads settled into domestic tranquility (of sorts) in a bungalow. Dagwood went to work for the world's most harried boss, and Blondie stayed home to raise the children. Alexander (nee Baby Dumpling) appeared in 1934 about the same time as Daisy, and Cookie a few years later, along with the pups.

Daisy is a small, bouncy dog with upraised tail and brows. Of her Young says:[12]

> I try to keep Daisy terribly interested in all the goings-on
> of the other people in the strip and she is terribly curious.
> Daisy thinks she is a person and reacts always as the human—
> BUT never talks . . . Occasionally, I use a question mark over
> her head in balloon form to indicate interest or curiosity
> and am always amused when I see the equivalent of our question
> mark over her head in foreign releases in Japanese, Spanish,
> Swedish, etc. Although I do not have the dogs speak, they laugh,
> cry, yell in pain, etc. as humans do. Somehow readers seem to
> accept that as natural. Of course, the Bumsteads all regard Daisy
> as one of the family.

Daisy is in on many of the family conspiracies to outwit poor Dagwood. Since Young won't let her talk, she makes an ideal conspirator. She listens to the plan, watches it succeed, and then often joins in the final guffaw, paw over mouth. Daisy is the only important comics canine who is female—and she is very feminine as Blondie pointed out to Dagwood in a recent Sunday adventure. After Dagwood failed in his brute-force methods of persuasion to get Daisy to wear her new checked coat, Blondie stepped in to talk softly of its chic look. Daisy paraded outside proudly, and Blondie told her hubby, "She may be a dog, but you have to treat her like a woman."

So Daisy is a step beyond Sandy. She is involved, if silent; however, compared to two of her contemporaries, Daisy is terribly traditional. She doesn't belong in the same kennel with either Snoopy or Otto.

Snoopy has been a regular in the Charles Schulz strip since it was launched in 1950, but it is hard to remember that he was once a dog. He walked on all fours, and he did not "think-talk" much less own a Wyeth (obtained after fire leveled his doghouse and destroyed his Van Gogh) or read Herman Hesse. Over the years, Snoopy changed from a dog (subhuman) to member of the Peanuts gang (human) to intellectual hedonist (superhuman). Even Schulz admits he doesn't know exactly how the transformation came about: [13]

> Snoopy's role in the strip has changed so gradually that I am frequently not aware as to exactly what has happened. For instance, I don't even remember how he got on top of the doghouse, but I do know that ideas seem to influence the drawing very much and that once you go a certain distance it is too late to back up. For instance, I never show Snoopy running on all four feet any more as a real dog might do, simply because I have gone beyond that point of no return.

One major turning point was when Snoopy started to do imitations. For months, he mimicked everything from alligators to mooses and, especially, vultures. After that, he seldom imitated a dog. Instead of just walking, he danced. ("To dance is to live." "Dancing is the highest form of art.") He skated; he donned dark glasses and became Joe Cool; he became the best baseball player (or at least Peppermint Patty thought that "funny looking kid with the big nose" was the best player on the team), and above all he became the relentless rival of the Red Baron.

His World War I flying ace bit became one of the most popular in the strip; however, the most amazing part of this fantasy is that Snoopy always loses. He, therefore, represents a sort of anti-hero. His doghouse/Sopwith Camel always goes down in flames, as he curses the Red Baron. We know that he will always be shot down, just as Charlie Brown will always fail at checkers, baseball, kite-flying, love and just about everything else. Most people resort to daydreams to succeed; Snoopy resorts to fantasy to fail.

Mort Walker's "Beatle Bailey" debuted in 1950, the same year as "Peanuts." Each now appears in about 1200 papers around the world, which puts them not too far behind the all-time champion, "Blondie." It was nearly a decade before Otto made his appearance.

As Walker wrote in 1971:[14]

> Otto first started appearing about 12 years ago as just a plain
> dog belonging to Sarge. He wore a sort of coverlet with S/Sgt.'s
> stripes on the sides. Then about a year or so ago, we decided
> to put Otto in uniform and make him really Sarge's pal and
> someone he could confide in. Otto was able to think and for
> a while he was talking sort of a garble. We scratched lines
> through the lettering in his balloons but still left the words
> readable. Although in uniform, Otto was not subject to army
> regulations and thus he was able to take his frustrations out
> on everyone from General Halftrack on down.

Otto is sometimes a super-soldier, scurrying around to salute
officers; at other times, he is a goof-off. He looks more and more
like Sarge, and usually serves as his alter ego, as in one strip when
Sarge was professing sorrow at sending Beetle and Killer out to stand
guard on a rainy night, and Otto gave away Sarge's innermost thoughts
by smiling and waving happily to them. Otto likes girls and civilian
comforts better than Sarge does, but at heart, he remains Sarge's
buddy. They often quaff a few beers or munch a pizza together.

It might appear from this that Snoopy and Otto are very much
alike; while both can talk and walk and hold their own among humans,
their philosophies and outlooks are quite different. Snoopy is a sophisti-
cate. He loves the finer things in life and spouts philosophy and if we
are to believe the interpretations of Robert Short, theology.[15] He
speaks French and even has his own pet bird, Woodstock. Snoopy
often has been called a hedonist, and indeed he concentrates on
bodily pleasures—most notably that old supper dish. He almost
always receives rather than gives. He doesn't even give away much
affection unless there is hope of getting something in return—and with
interest. Note, however, Snoopy's role with Woodstock. He accom-
panies him southward, even sharing a nest with him for the night.
("I feel like such a fool.") Woodstock gets the best of Snoopy, and
Snoopy simply accepts that as the nature of things; he certainly does
not display that attitude toward any of the humans in the strip. Otto
is more low brow, like the milieu of the barracks. It is hard to imagine
him with a pet. He is, literally, one of the boys—a hail fellow well met.
Otto sponges whatever he can get, unashamedly and openly.

Their antropomorphic change has been so marked that readers
probably do not think of either Snoopy or Otto as dogs anymore.
That removes them from the normal constraints on the roles in which

humans are willing to accept dogs. Dogs are all right, you know, as long as they know their place.

From this survey of the various media, it is clear why the dog is so often elevated by man to hero status. The good dog serves as a foil to his master, is fiercely loyal to his master, and protects his master. The dog is a hero, not because of his animal characteristics, but because he is a good nigger.

NOTES

[1] Edward Wagenknecht, *The Movies in the Age of Innocence* (Norman: University of Oklahoma Press, 1962), p. 48.

[2] Roger Boussinot, *L'Encyclopedie du Cinema* (Paris: Bordas, 1967), p. 1278.

[3] Bosley Crowther, *The Lion's Share* (New York: E.P. Dutton, 1957), pp. 279-280.

[4] Jim Harmon, *The Great Radio Heroes* (New York: Ace Books, 1967), p. 210.

[5] George W. Trendle interview, Detroit, April 11, 1969.

[6] Mary Jane Higby, *Tune In Tomorrow* (New York: Ace Books, 1968), pp. 161-167.

[7] See, for example, Coulton Waugh, *The Comics* (New York: Macmillan, 1947); Stephen Becker, *Comic Art in America* (New York: Simon & Schuster, 1959); George Perry and Alan Aldredge, *The Penguin Book of the Comics*, Rev. ed. (Middlesex, England: Penguin Books Ltd., 1971); Pierre Couperie and Maurice C. Horn, *A History of the Comic Strip* (New York: Crown Publishers, 1968).

[8] Maurice Horn, *75 Years of the Comics*, (Boston: Boston Book & Art, 1971), introduction.

[9] Maria Leach, *God Had a Dog: Folklore of the Dog* (New Brunswick: Rutgers University Press, 1961). There are 537 motifs on dogs in Stith Thompson, *Motif-Index of Folk Literature*, 2d ed. (Bloomington: Indiana University Press, 1955-58.)

[10] Waugh, *The Comics*, p. 151.

[11] Katherine M. Wolf and Marjorie Fiske, "The Children Talk About Comics," in Paul E. Lazarsfeld and Frank M. Stanton, *Communications Research 1948-1949* (New York: Harper and Brothers, 1949), p. 11.

[12] Young to Author, Oct. 13, 1971.

[13] Schulz to Author, Nov. 2, 1971.

[14] Walker to Author, Oct. 12, 1971.

[15] Robert Short, *The Gospel According to Peanuts* (Richmond, Va.: John Knox Press, 1964).

By RAY B. BROWNE
Epilogue

The need for the existence of the hero and heroine in American democratic society presents a paradox which has always puzzled thoughtful people. And, as made perfectly clear in the preceding essays, we as a people have reacted in several ways.

No American ever pondered the question more than Herman Melville did. Examining the apparent irresistible urge to heroize he demonstrated that men's and women's heroes and heroines are men and women themselves. Ishmael—not Ahab—is the hero of *Moby Dick*. Ishmael is the common sailor who wants to sail before the mast. Thus he is not the conventional hero, and in him Melville anticipated in a very real way by many years America's drive to create the hero as anti-hero, not as superbigman but as verylittleguy. But Melville was no sexist. His reverence was for humanity, not men or women but both. In one of his short stories, "Norfolk Isle and the Chola Widow," he created Hunilla the anti-heroine as heroine as one of his richest and most moving portraits.

Melville, however, recognized that myth and the urge to heroize seem to be profoundly a part of man's nature and will persist no matter how strong the forces working against them. One would think that no stronger force could work against them than television. To paraphrase Napoleon, no man is a hero to the TV tube, or indeed *on* it. But the medium's workers, needing to justify their existence and apparently recognizing the need of people, endeavor constantly to create heroes and heroines, working against reality to picture a world as false as that in *The Song of Roland* or the King Arthur stories. There is perhaps no more striking example of man's unceasing desire to idealize the real world than his effort to manipulate the TV screen to make events appear bigger than life.

In *Bury My Heart at Wounded Knee* (1972) author Dee Brown says that there are no heroes any more in this world. But he is correct only if one equates heroes with giants. There are no more giants on the earth (if indeed there ever were), but heroes and heroines there are, as the selections in this volume thoroughly indicate. Giants these heroes and heroines are not—in the conventional sense of that word. But they serve exactly the same purpose heroes and the heroic have always served—as a bar on which men and women can chin their aspirations and dreams—can stretch and try to become less human and more godlike. Camelot has deteriorated into Ghettoland, Galahad has become a crooked politician, the American Dream has become manifestly a nightmare, and Americans one and all recognize that it is no longer possible to move to the West and on to Heaven.

But they keep trying. They want to experience life as bigger than actuality, realizing simultaneously that perhaps it is in fact just as small. With this comprehension America may at last have understood, as Melville said about Hawthorne's truth, that though you may be "witched" by the apparent sunlight, "there is the blackness beyond," and one must recognize this before he or she is able to free himself or herself from fear. It is basically fear that makes men and women create heroes and heroines. Once they have purged themselves of that fear, the compulsion to heroize may be a past nightmare. Until then, however, the need is very much with us. Studying it can only cast light into shadow. It is hoped that the essays in this collection have cast a great deal of light and understanding. The editors of this volume are acutely aware that most of the essays study men and the hero. No sexist bias was intended. Feeling that women and the heroine should perhaps at this stage be presented by women, a companion volume, *Images of Women In Fiction: Feminist Perspectives*, edited by Susan Cornillon, will soon be published by this Press. The two volumes will present American society with some thoroughness and truth.

With greater awareness of themselves, the world around them and their own needs and drives, maybe men and women can rise— Ishmael-like or Hunilla-like—from the vortex of experience and, as Melville's hero and heroine did, live to tell the tale.

CONTRIBUTORS

Bruce E. Coad is Chairman of the English Department, Tarrant County Junior College District, Fort Worth, Texas.

Ronald R. Cummings is in the English Department, Purdue University.

Anthony Hopkins is on the English faculty, Glendon College, York University, Toronto, Canada.

Patricia Kane is on the English faculty of Macalester College, St. Paul, Minn.

Bruce Lohof is on the History faculty and director of American Studies, University of Miami, Florida.

Fred MacFadden is on the faculty of Coppin State College, Baltimore, Md.

Marshall McLuhan is Director of the Center for Technology and Culture at Toronto University.

Michael H. Mehlman is Chief Casework Supervisor, Social Services, Lake County Welfare Department, Painesville, Ohio.

Gerard O'Connor is on the faculty of Lowell Technological Institute, Lowell, Mass.

H. D. Piper is on the English faculty, Southern Illinois University, Carbondale.

Jerome L. Rodnitzky is Associate Professor of History, University of Texas, Arlington.

Leverett T. Smith, Jr. is on the English faculty, Alliance College, Cambridge, Pa.

John D. Stevens is Associate Professor of Journalism, University of Michigan.

David Stupple is on the sociology faculty at Eastern Michigan University.

EDITORS

Ray B. Browne is Director of the Center for the Study of Popular Culture, Bowling Green University, Bowling Green, Ohio.

Marshall Fishwick is Director of the American Studies Institute, Lincoln University, Pa.

Michael T. Marsden is co-editor of the *Journal of Popular Film* and on the faculty of the Center for the Study of Popular Culture, Bowling Green University, Bowling Green, Ohio.

EDITORS

Ray B. Browne is Director of the Center for the Study of Popular Culture, Bowling Green University, Bowling Green, Ohio.

Marshall Fishwick is Professor in the Humanities, Lincoln University, Pa.

Michael T. Marsden is co-editor of the Journal of Popular Film and on the Faculty of the Center for the Study of Popular Culture, Bowling Green University, Bowling Green, Ohio.